Getting the Best Equipment Lease Deal

Getting the Best Equipment Lease Deal

An Equipment Leasing Guide for Business Lessees

Richard M. Contino

BEP BUSINESS EXPERT PRESS

Getting the Best Equipment Lease Deal: An Equipment Leasing Guide for Business Lessees

Copyright © Business Expert Press, LLC, 2020.

Cover image licensed by Ingram Image, StockPhotoSecrets.com

First published in 2020 by
Business Expert Press, LLC
222 East 46th Street, New York, NY 10017
www.businessexpertpress.com

ISBN-13: 978-1-94999-196-3 (paperback)
ISBN-13: 978-1-94999-197-0 (e-book)

Business Expert Press Business Law and Corporate Risk Management Collection

Collection ISSN: 2333-6722 (print)
Collection ISSN: 2333-6730 (electronic)

Cover and interior design by Exeter Premedia Services Private Ltd., Chennai, India

First edition: 2020

10 9 8 7 6 5 4 3 2 1

Printed in the United States of America.

Dedication

To Penelope, May-Lynne, and Matthew

Abstract

This book is a guidebook for any business, small to large, considering acquiring equipment through a leasing alternative. It explains the pros and cons of leasing equipment, as well as how leasing and financing companies operate and the pitfalls to watch out for, provides guidance on how to financially evaluate lease offers and compare them to other financing alternatives. It also discusses the various business, accounting, and tax implications. Included are practical tips, recommendations and strategies for getting the best lease deal, a legal and business explanation of all relevant documents, and strategies to negotiate the relevant documents to get the best terms. Very simply, this book is a comprehensive guidebook tailored expressly for the business lessee—with up-to-date suggestions, insider tips, and observations. So, if you're thinking about leasing equipment and want to know how to negotiate the best possible lease deal, this book is for you.

Keywords

equipment financing; equipment leasing; leasing; financing; leasing deal; lease agreements; product financing agreements; lease versus buy decisions

Contents

Contents

Introduction

This book is a guidebook for any business, small to large, considering acquiring equipment through a leasing alternative. It explains the pros and cons of leasing equipment, as well as how leasing and financing companies operate and the pitfalls to watch out for, provides guidance on how to financially evaluate lease offers and compare them to other financing alternatives. It also discusses the various business, accounting, and tax implications. Included are practical tips, recommendations, and strategies for getting the best lease deal; a legal and business explanation of all relevant documents; and strategies to negotiate the relevant documents to get the best terms. Very simply, this book is a comprehensive guidebook tailored expressly for the business lessee—with up-to-date suggestions, insider tips, and observations.

So, if you are considering leasing needed equipment and you want to have the best available leasing information to enable you to get the best possible lease deal, this book is for you. It will, for example, address issues such as:

- How does the leasing marketplace really work?
- How does a leasing company operate?
- What are the leasing profit areas?
- When is leasing a poor choice?
- What is the best way for a company to solicit lease bids?
- Does a lease financing proposal letter really commit a lessor?
- When will a lease meet the Internal Revenue Service (IRS) requirements?
- Can a fixed price purchase option be used?
- How should a lease be analyzed financially?
- What impact do the new lease accounting rules have?

Unfortunately, because of the many variables that can be involved in a lease decision, the desirability of leasing for, and the lease evaluation criteria used by, one company may be totally inappropriate for another company. This book will, however, provide the reader with a comprehensive working knowledge of the fundamental tools necessary to competently handle any lease situation from start to finish. The relevant issues that must be taken into account in developing a solid financing approach will be identified, described, and explained.

Here is some of what you will find:

Proposal stage: In any lease financing arrangement, the proposal stage is the critical point when the parties establish the transaction's business parameters. At this stage, you, as a prospective lessee, are in your strongest negotiating position. By taking advantage of some simple techniques recommended by the author, you can, for example, get a *below market* lease rent.

Documentation: The documentation stage—where your leasing rights and obligations are defined—is another crucial step in the transaction. To be fully aware of what the document risks and obligations are is essential to ensure that the terms and conditions of your lease deal work for you. For example, if you inadvertently assume certain state tax payment obligations, your effective cost of leasing equipment can dramatically increase.

Tax issues: Problems often arise because of lack of understanding of the complex leasing tax issues. If the IRS tax rules are violated, the desired tax benefits treatment may be lost. The original tax guidelines promulgated in 1975 have been restated in two more recent revenue procedures, discussed and explained.

Accounting issues: How a lease must be accounted for should always be a foremost consideration. Improper structuring can cause undesirable accounting treatment. The Financial Accounting Standards Board has promulgated an extensive and complicated set of rules on accounting for leases, which have recently been revised. The existing rules are explained and put into a meaningful and current context for a lessee.

Financial issues: Another key consideration is the financial side of a lease decision. There are many apparent—and some not so apparent—economic advantages and disadvantages to leasing. A prospective lessee can end up making the wrong financing decision by using an incorrect method of analysis. The economic advantages and disadvantages, as well as the methods of financial analysis, are explained so that you as a prospective lessee can determine what your position is or should be.

The business of leasing equipment: How does a lessor reduce their risks and make money in the leasing business? Surprisingly, it is often in ways that are not readily apparent. And, for a prospective lessee, understanding how a lessor makes money will increase its negotiating leverage.

In summary, this book gives the reader a complete grasp of the legal, financial, tax, accounting, and business considerations for leasing, including those that are necessary to evaluate and negotiate the most favorably structured equipment leasing transaction.

Richard M. Contino, Esq.

CHAPTER 1

Equipment Leasing Fundamentals for Business Lessees

Overview

The concept of the lease as a property right, and the rights and duties of lessors and lessees, has been part of our legal tradition for decades, particularly in the case of real estate. Leasing began to emerge in the 1950s as a viable alternative for acquiring equipment. At the time of this writing, the latest available annual (2017) business statistics from the Equipment Leasing and Finance Foundation show that businesses acquired 1.7 trillion U.S. dollar of equipment and software, 60 percent of which, or over one trillion U.S. dollars, was financed with leasing (48 percent of this total), the most common method, followed by lines of credit (9 percent of this total), and secured loans (8 percent of this total). So, there is no doubt that the equipment leasing industry plays a major role in the financial community. An equipment user can lease virtually any type of equipment on a variety of terms.

Notwithstanding the many benefits for an equipment user, there have been some drawbacks to equipment leasing. The legal requirements and financial considerations are, at times, extremely complex and the lease documents are often difficult for business people to understand. Because of intense competition among leasing companies for business, however, some progress has been made favoring equipment lessees—for example, many leasing companies now provide lease documents written in plain English, so they are more readily understandable by the layperson.

The interest in leasing as an alternative means of acquiring equipment, however, continues to prompt a deluge of questions from equipment users. For example:

- What are the tax advantages and disadvantages to the lessee?
- What is the best business structure for a lease?
- How should a lease transaction be analyzed from a financial viewpoint?
- How are leases treated for accounting purposes?
- What are the leasing risks, and what are the benefits?

For these, and many other questions, there are no easy answers, but if your company is considering leasing equipment, the material in this book will give you a solid basis to reach a decision and put you in the best position to negotiate the best possible lease deal.

What Type of Businesses Can Benefit from Leasing Equipment?

In general, any equipment user can benefit from a properly negotiated equipment lease arrangement, whether it is a multinational corporation, a small, privately held or family-owned business, or an individual using equipment for business reasons. Whether or not an equipment user in a particular situation should generally lease equipment they need, however, depends on a variety of factors that vary with each situation, outlined in The Pros and Cons of Leasing for a Business Lessee following.

Who Are the Potential Lessors?

In theory, any company in the financing business can be a potential lessor of equipment. However, because of the competitive nature of equipment leasing and the specialized expertise required, only certain types of organizations are actively in the leasing market.

For discussion purposes, it is useful to separate the potential lessors into five categories: individuals, independent leasing companies, lease brokers, captive leasing companies, and banks. If you are considering leasing equipment, you will find an understanding of the categories help-ful in narrowing the field of potential lessors.

Wealthy Individuals

Prior to the 1986 Tax Reform Act (TRA), the role of the wealthy indi-vidual as lessor was limited because of the rules restricting an individ-ual from claiming investment tax credits (ITCs) on leased property. Now that the ITC is not currently available to lessors, except in limited equipment categories, wealthy individuals can be more rate competi-tive. This coupled with the fact that they often will take greater business risks than a traditional leasing company can make them a good choice in difficult financing situations. In this regard, a few innovative equip-ment leasing companies and investment bankers have developed over the years interesting investment programs for individuals who have made them, at times, a part of the equipment financing business. For example, some railcar brokers set up individual investor programs that provide wealthy individuals with opportunities to invest in short-term railcar leases.

> **Recommendation:** If you are a prospective lessee considering leasing from an individual, you must look at more than any rent advantage. For example, because individuals often take aggressive tax positions, they may run afoul of the income tax laws. The Internal Revenue Service may then put a lien on all the individ-ual's property, including the leased equipment. Also, individuals can be somewhat more arbitrary to deal with when variances from the lease terms are required.

Independent Leasing Companies

Independent leasing companies, often referred to as third-party leas-ing companies, provide a major source of equipment lease financing. Because leasing is their principal source of revenue, in today's compet-itive market, independent leasing companies are extremely aggressive and, in some cases, are willing to risk bending the tax rules for the lessee's benefit to win a transaction. For example, some will give a lessee the right to buy the equipment at a low predetermined fixed price when the lease ends—a practice that can have adverse tax consequences (see Chapter 5).

There are two basic types of independent leasing companies: those that merely buy and lease equipment to the equipment user (*finance leasing companies*), the vast majority of the independent leasing companies, and those that also offer other services, such as the maintenance and repair of the equipment leased (*service leasing companies*).

Finance Leasing Companies

Finance leasing companies, lessors of multimillions of dollars of equipment each year, operate in much the same manner as banks or other financing companies. They do not maintain an equipment inventory, but rather, after agreeing to a lease with a prospective lessee, buy the specific equipment needed for the lease. In this case, the prospective lessee orders the needed equipment from the equipment vendor and assigns the right, but not the obligation, to buy the equipment to the leasing company. When the equipment arrives, if it is in acceptable condition and is accepted by the equipment user under the lease contract, the leasing company pays for it and takes title to the equipment.

Finance leasing companies typically write financial-type leases, referred to as finance leases, that run, generally, from 70 to 80 percent of the equipment's useful life. The total amount received under these leases, from the rents payable and the equipment end-of-lease (residual) value proceeds (taking into account, possibly, any available equipment ownership tax benefits), is sufficient to provide the lessor with a full return of their equipment investment and a profit. If the equipment purchase is leveraged with third-party debt (a leverage lease arrangement), the rents will also cover the full repayment of the debt. This type of long-term lease is net to the lessee. That is, the lessee must assume substantially all the equipment ownership responsibilities, such as maintenance, taxes, and insurance.

Service Leasing Companies

Service leasing companies provide nonfinancial services to lessees in addition to the equipment financing. Services may include equipment maintenance and repair or advice on the equipment's operation and design. Service leases have become increasingly popular for prospective lessees.

Service lessors typically limit their activity to a single type of equipment, such as computers, or to a single type of industry, such as the mining industry. The intense experience gained through equipment or industry specialization enables them to reduce many leasing risks. For example, because of a specialized equipment focus, they often are able to deal effectively with equipment when it comes off lease, which, in turn, reduces their end-of-lease equipment re-leasing or sale risk. And, because of that reduced risk, they will often offer attractive lease termination or equipment exchange privileges.

> **Observation:** Many industry participants believe that product specialization is less risky for a lessor than industry specialization because there is a greater likelihood that an industry specialized lessor would suffer more if their industry hits hard times than an equipment specialized lessor would if one of the industries in which their equipment was used hit hard times.

Service lessors often write leases with much shorter lease terms than finance leases, referred to as non-payout leases. Because of the non-payout nature, the lease rents will typically not recoup for the lessor its entire equipment investment during the first lease term. And, to recover its investment and make a profit, the service lessor must continue to re-lease the equipment. If the equipment becomes obsolete sooner than expected, the lessor may incur a loss. So, to be compensated for taking this risk, and for providing other services, service lessors will generally charge higher rents than finance lessors, the amount of which is often buried in *package* payments that include the rental charge for the equipment and the payment of services provided.

When should a prospective lessee consider using a service leasing company? Basically, when the lessee needs the specialized services offered by the service lessor or wants a shorter lease term or early termination rights. An equipment user, for example, may want a shorter term when there is a high risk of equipment obsolescence or where the user's industry is cyclic.

> **Recommendation:** If you are considering leasing equipment that your company may want to return early, a comparison should be made of any higher rents typically payable under a shorter-term lease offered by a service lessor against the lower rents, and early termination penalty, typically payable under a longer-term finance lease offered by finance lessors with an early termination right. Frequently, the short-term service lease is economically preferable, because finance lease termination penalties are often substantial.

Lease Brokers

Also referred to as *lease underwriters* or *syndicators*, lease brokers package lease transactions for the account of third parties. Put simply, they match up prospective lessees with prospective lessor-investors. They charge a fee for their service—usually ranging from 0.75 to 8 percent of the leased equipment's cost, typically paid for by the lessor-investors, but often indirectly by the lessee because it is typically built into the rent charges.

To put the lease broker's role into perspective, it is helpful to understand how a broker normally operates. Generally, a lease broker begins by contacting all types of equipment users and vendors to determine whether they have any leasing needs. In the case of a prospective lessee, they will define the rough leasing parameters through discussions with the prospective lessee. At this juncture, the broker may perform a very preliminary credit check on the prospective lessee to make sure their credit condition is marketable. If there are not any problems, the broker will formulate a concise lease structure, including rental rate, and offer it to the equipment user, generally through a formal proposal letter.

If the equipment user finds the proposed arrangement acceptable, the broker then proceeds to find prospective lessor-investors, commonly referred to as equity or investor participants, which in the case of smaller transactions, is often an independent leasing company. If the transaction is to be leveraged with third-party debt, a leveraged lease, it may also put out feelers for prospective lenders, commonly referred to as debt participants. In the case of larger (multimillion dollar) transactions, the debt side is usually handled by an investment banker. Once the lease broker locates the equity and, if applicable, the debt participants, the broker proceeds to shepherd the transaction through documentation to completion.

Although generally acting exclusively as a broker, a lease underwriter may, on occasion, invest some of its own funds in the equipment along with other third-party lessor-investors and, thereby, become a part owner. By doing so, the lease underwriter can add credibility to the investment and thus be able to sell the lease transaction to potential investors more readily.

One of a lease broker's major assets is its knowledge of, and contacts in, the leasing and banking industry. Because a lease broker is continually in the market, they know where to find competitive, cooperative, and realistic equity and debt participants. And, they will also know how to get the equity participants to agree to meet a lessee's needs, including, for example, on lease rates, overall transaction structure, and documentation.

Recommendations:

- If you are considering a finance lease arrangement, particularly in the case of a multimillion dollars lease transaction, you should invite one or more top lease brokers to participate, in addition to regular leasing companies, because of their ability to effectively structure lease offers that fit a lessee's needs and find aggressive lessor-investors.
- Because of the risk that any lease broker you want to work with cannot perform as promised, requiring you to have to start looking again for financing, put a realistic performance time limit on any broker you use and plan for any non-performance possibilities by, for example, having a backup leasing company ready in the event there is a funding problem.

Captive Leasing Companies

A relative few equipment vendors have set up their own leasing companies, generally referred to as captive leasing companies, to service their customers. Although the purpose is usually to offer lease financing on equipment sold by an affiliated company, some captive leasing companies also may be willing to buy and lease equipment sold by a nonaffiliated company, particularly if it includes equipment sold by its affiliate.

A captive leasing company marketing an affiliated company's equipment can often offer attractive rates because its affiliated company will make an equipment sale profit, thus enabling the captive lessor to work with a lower financing profit than other types of lessors. Coupled with its knowledge of the equipment's potential residual value, this can result in attractive rents for a lessee.

> **Recommendation:** In connection with any equipment vendor you are dealing with, determine if the vendor has a captive leasing company and, if so, ask the vendor's captive leasing company to submit a lease quotation for several reasons; their lease rate may be very low, and their documentation may be simple.

Banks

Many banks, particularly national banks, are actively involved in equipment leasing. This is less so for regional and community banks because of their general lack of equipment leasing expertise. The banks usually offer only net finance leases because of regulatory requirements and because these types of leases provide the least risk and most similarity to their lending activity.

Banks generally do not take aggressive equipment residual value positions, thus resulting in potentially higher market lease rates (that is, more of their principal investment must be recouped in the lease rents, a concept explained in Chapter 2). However, their cost of funds in many cases is lower than that of nonbank lessors, often offsetting any conservative residual value positions.

The terms and rates offered by bank lessors often vary significantly from one transaction to the next over a period of time. Internal bank policies may contribute to that variation. Banks are not as dependent as most non-bank lessors on their leasing activities for revenues, and so, many can afford to miss out on deals. Periodically, however, they can go on major drives for lease business and, at those times, they can be extremely rate aggressive.

There is a hidden risk in dealing with banks. Because leasing is not considered their main line of business, if they experience general financial difficulties, as they have in the late 1980s and early 1990s, their leasing department is usually one of the first to go. Management's rationale is that they must go back to basics to get their financial house in order. Chase Manhattan Bank's sale of their profitable leasing subsidiaries in 1991 is a good example of what can happen when a bank experiences general financial problems.

It is worth mentioning that banks directly participate in the leasing market in another major way; they frequently act as lenders in leveraged lease transactions.

> **Recommendation:** Given the unpredictability of bank lessors' responses to potential lease transactions and their commitment to the business, you should not rely exclusively on one bank to service all your company's financing needs, unless, possibly, they have a robust equipment leasing activity.

Types of Leases and Financing Arrangements Available

As suggested earlier, the leasing of equipment is a well-accepted way for businesses to acquire needed equipment. A lease is simply a contract where the owner of equipment, the lessor, agrees to let a company in need of the equipment, the lessee, use the equipment for an agreed-upon period, the lease term, and lease payment. At the end of the lease term, the lessee returns the equipment to the lessor.

Although the concept of a lease is simple, the lease documents, however, can often be complex and needs to be fully understood to get the best lease deal. Additionally, there are many lease arrangement variations, some of which affect only the lessor, which will be discussed next. The lease document itself is discussed in detail in Chapter 9.

In addition to financing equipment under a lease arrangement, there are other equipment and product financing arrangements that allow businesses to acquire the needed equipment or other products, without having to pay the full product purchase price upfront. Equipment can be financed using a rental arrangement, which, in effect, is the same as a lease arrangement, often for a short term, also at times referred to as an operating lease arrangement. In addition, equipment or other product acquisitions can be financed using a conditional sale arrangement, essentially a form of debt financing, where the product user pays a specific periodic payment, such as monthly, over the financing term and at the end of the financing term, owns the product free and clear. Interestingly, a conditional sale financing can be set up using a lease agreement by simply giving the lessee the option to purchase the product at the end of the lease term for one U.S. dollar. And, as discussed earlier, there are also service leases where some form of service is supplied along with the equipment. Other financing examples would be when product financing is arranged through what are referred to as managed services or fee-per-use agreements, discussed later in this chapter, where equipment along with related services, such as maintenance or repair services, or supplies, such as disposables used with the equipment, are provided for an agreed-upon term and periodic payment. Similar in general concept to services leases provided by service lessors, the latter two types of acquisition arrangements are relatedly recent structures, typically, for obvious reasons, offered only by product vendors with the capability of supplying collateral services, supplies, or other non-equipment offerings.

Finally, there are two basic lease variations: a leveraged lease (typically only used for multimillion dollar transactions), where the lessor borrows a portion of the equipment cost from a third-party lender, and a non-leveraged lease, where the lessor pays for the equipment entirely with their own funds.

Long-Term Lease: The Finance Lease

A common type of equipment lease used by leasing companies, bank— and non-bank-affiliated, is a finance lease. These leases are considered long-term leases because the primary, or main, lease term usually runs for most of the equipment's useful life. Typically, the total cash flow over the primary term, from rents, tax savings, and the end-of-lease equipment re-sale or re-lease (residual) value, will be sufficient to pay back the lessor's investment, take care of its administrative expenses, pay off any equipment-related debt obligations and commissions, and provide a profit. Because they are entered into by lessors as long-term financial commitments, finance lessors usually impose a substantial prepayment penalty for any lessee's early lease termination right in an amount that will assure the lessor of a return of its investment and a profit, at least up to the date of termination.

Consistent with its financial nature, a finance lease is usually a net lease in which the fundamental ownership responsibilities, such as maintaining and repairing the equipment, paying for the necessary insurance, and taking care of property, use, and sales taxes, are placed on the lessee. A net finance lease can be compared to an equipment loan, in that the lessor, like a lender, is involved only in asset funding, responsible only to pay for the equipment, lease it to the lessee for the agreed-upon term and not interfere with its use.

Because a finance lease's term runs for most of the equipment's useful life, the lessee, in effect, bears most of the risk of the equipment becoming obsolete. The degree of obsolescence risk that the finance lessor assumes depends on the equipment's anticipated end-of-lease term, or residual, value. If, for example, a lessor computes the rent based on a zero-equipment residual value at the lease term's end, the lessor has no residual value risk and, thus, no obsolescence risk. This, of course, presumes there is no premature equipment return as a result, for instance, of a lessee default. As a practical matter, however, a lessor must generally use a residual value greater than zero to be price competitive, particularly in larger transactions. The risk of obsolescence is then on the lessor to the extent of the value estimated. If its profit is in part dependent on the anticipated residual value, the greater the risk of obsolescence the greater the chance the transaction will not turn out to be as profitable as anticipated.

One of a financial lessor's principal concerns is the protection of their investment in the event of a lease default or an equipment casualty. Toward this end, finance leases usually include provisions to make the lessor whole if any of these events occur. From a casualty loss standpoint, the lease may include what are often referred to as a stipulated loss value provisions, requiring the lessee to pay the lessor an amount of money if an equipment casualty occurs, determined based on when the casualty occurs. The stipulated loss value amount guarantees the lessor a return of their outstanding investment, reimburses them for any tax benefit losses, and assures them of at least some of its anticipated profit. The stipulated loss values are also sometimes used as a measure of lease default damages, although there are other methods for measuring default damages. The same approach is true for lease default damage provisions, which contain default damage formulas that build in a return of the lessor outstanding investment, reimburse them for any tax benefit losses, and assure them of at least some of its anticipated profit.

Finance leases frequently contain a *hell or high-water* rent commitment. Under this type of obligation, a lessee must pay the full rent when due unconditionally and cannot reduce the amount paid even though they have a legitimate claim against the lessor for money owed. This is not as bad as it sounds for a lessee, because they can still bring a lawsuit against the lessor for any claims.

The hell or high-water rent provision is critical for a finance lessor to have in a leverage lease transaction, where they want to borrow money on a nonrecourse loan basis to purchase the equipment. *Reason:* In a nonrecourse loan, the lender agrees to look only to the lessee's rent payments and the equipment for a return of its investment. With a hell or high-water provision, the lender need not be concerned that a dispute between the lessor and the lessee will result in the lessee's withholding rent.

Short-Term Lease: The Operating Lease

Where a lease's primary term is significantly shorter than the equipment's useful life, the lease is often referred to as an operating lease, a term not to be confused with the term as used for accounting classification. Operating leases typically run anywhere from a few months to a few years, although some are as short as a few days.

Because the lease terms are relatively short, an operating lessor usually cannot earn much of their equipment investment back through the rents from one lease transaction. Thus, they must either sell or re-lease the equipment on attractive terms to come out ahead. The danger to an operating lessor, of course, is that the equipment's market value will be inadequate to allow it to sell or re-lease it on economically favorable terms. In other words, it has the risk of equipment obsolescence. As a result, such a lessor will attempt to earn their money back faster to lessen its investment exposure by charging a higher rent than in a finance lease.

Their short-lease terms and easy cancelation provisions make operating leases attractive to equipment users in several situations. One is where the user anticipates using the equipment only for a short time, such as with certain types of rail cars. Another is where the user wants to be able to change equipment if something better comes out. For this reason, users often lease computer equipment under operating leases because of constant technological improvements.

The Leverage Lease

A leveraged lease is a lease where a percentage of the funds to buy the equipment, usually 60 to 80 percent, is loaned to the lessor by a bank or other lender. Because the lessor has put up only a small percentage of the equipment's cost, their investment is said to be leveraged because its economic return is based on 100 percent of the cost. Leveraging generally enables a lessor to provide a lessee with relatively lower rents, while at the same time, maintaining their return. Many multimillion-dollar net finance leases are often structured as leveraged leases.

The debt used to leverage a lease transaction is usually nonrecourse debt, with the lender having no recourse against the lessor for loan nonpayment and only looking to the rental stream, the lessee, and the value of the equipment for its repayment. In such an arrangement, the lessor must assign to the lender its rights under the lease, including the right to the rental payments and provide a lien on the equipment.

> **Observation:** While a lessor has no repayment obligations to a nonrecourse lender if the lessee defaults, they do bear some risk because their rights against the lessee and the equipment are subordinated to the lender's repayment rights.

The Non-Leveraged Lease

Also referred to as an unleveraged or straight lease, a non-leveraged lease is the one in which the lessor pays for the equipment from entirely their own funds. Leasing companies often enter into non-leveraged leases, particularly in the case of transactions under one million U.S. dollars.

The advantage to using a non-leveraged lease structure is that there are only two principals involved in the actual financing, the lessee and the lessor. Because of the limited number of parties, the mechanics of putting together a transaction are simpler, saving time and documentation costs, such as legal fees. One disadvantage for a lessee, however, is that the rent is usually higher than it would be if the lease were leveraged.

The Service Lease

Leases in which the lessor assumes some equipment ownership responsibilities, such as maintenance, repair, insurance, or recordkeeping, in addition to providing asset financing, are usually called service leases. Service leases generally had relatively short lease terms, although, today, service leases are increasingly being offered with longer terms because of equipment user requests.

Managed Services Agreements

A managed services agreement generally provides a customer with bundled equipment and services for an agreed-upon term, ranging from 5 to 20 years. Managed Services Agreements are often used with energy-saving offerings where the services provider provides energy-saving equipment and related services, such as maintenance, as well as other collateral services, for a bundled stated price, but they are also increasingly used in connection with providing technology and medical equipment and related services. Customers favor this type of agreement because there is a possibility the payment obligations will be treated as off-balance sheet obligations if the new accounting rules, discussed in Chapter 8, do not dictate otherwise and, accordingly, if treated as an off-balance sheet item, the contract will not adversely affect their financial ratios for borrowing purposes. For the customer, using managed services agreements can eliminate, or reduce, needs for internal service staffing.

Fee-Per-Use Agreements

A fee-per-use agreement is another potentially *off-balance sheet* service-type contract gaining popularity, particularly in the medical field, assuming, again, that the new accounting rules, discussed in Chapter 8, do not dictate otherwise. Under this type of contract, the product vendor typically supplies a customer with the product vendor's equipment for an agreed-upon term and imposes a charge for the equipment generally on the basis of the amount of vendor-provided supplies or disposables used in connection with the equipment operation, often obligating the customer to a minimum periodic supply or disposable use over the contract term.

Leasing's Tax Motivations

The General Equipment Tax Picture

The tax aspects of equipment leasing are addressed in Chapters 4 and 5, but a brief overview will be helpful in gaining a full understanding of what is often an important aspect of leasing equipment, the equipment ownership tax benefits, essentially equipment depreciation and, to a very limited extent, available investment tax credits.

Although any type of equipment can be leased, the critical question for a prospective lessee taking into account the available equipment ownership tax benefits is at what cost? While the answer is complex, as a threshold matter, leasing often is not the lowest cost way for a company able to use equipment ownership tax benefits to acquire equipment, unless the lessor can take advantage of certain tax benefits and indirectly pass them on, at least in part, in the form of relatively lower lease rents, and, in addition, assumes that a portion of its investment will be returned by selling or re-leasing the leased equipment at lease end if it is not purchased or re-leased by the lessee. Looking first at the tax benefit issue, consider the following hypothetical example.

Illustrative example: *The tax advantage*: Company Able wants to acquire the use of a 20,000 U.S. dollar truck. It can borrow funds from its bank for five years at the prime rate, assumed for this example to be 10 percent a year. If Company Able were able to borrow 100 percent of the funds required, its cost to finance the truck would be the cost of the 20,000 U.S. dollars loan.

As an alternative, Company Able could lease the truck from Company Baker. Assume Company Baker also borrowed *at prime* from the same bank, and that it would fund the truck purchase entirely from its bank borrowing. If there were no truck owner- ship tax advantages, the only way it could make a profit would be to charge a lease rate greater than its cost of funds. Thus, Com- pany Able would have to pay something over the prime rate to Company Baker, a not very attractive arrangement.

Although the preceding example is admittedly oversimplified and not completely realistic, it makes the point—when the lessor and the lessee have the same borrowing rate capabilities, leasing may not be the most economical way for a lessee to acquire equipment it needs, unless the les- sor is able to use available equipment ownership tax benefits, takes them into account as a lease profit ingredient, and passes them on to a lessee though relative rental rate reductions, and the prospective lessee cannot use some or all of the ownership tax benefits. How this actually works is explained later in this book.

The Equipment Ownership Tax Benefit

What tax benefits are available to the lessor from equipment ownership? As you will learn in Chapter 4, the significant tax benefits for the lessor today from equipment ownership are basically the depreciation deduc- tions available under the tax rules and, in limited cases, what are referred to as energy tax credits.

Under the tax depreciation rules, a lessor generally can write off their equipment's costs over a period significantly shorter than the equipment's useful life and at an accelerated rate. In a typical lease, the lessor's deduc- tions in the early years will exceed the rental income, permitting the lessor to offset other income with those excess deductions. If an energy tax credit is available, the lessor gets a dollar-for-dollar deduction to their income tax liability for the amount of the energy tax credit.

The Lessee's Tax Consequences

Basically, an equipment user decreases their tax benefits by becoming a lessee rather than an equipment owner. As lessee, however, the user can deduct their rental payments, but those will typically be less than the depreciation they could have deducted in earlier years. Then, why should leasing be considered? As it turns out, there are many other financial and business reasons for a prospective lessee to lease rather than buy, discussed next. And, in addition, leasing is particularly attractive to equipment users who cannot take timely advantage of all of the equipment ownership tax benefits. Two types of users basically fall into this category: those who have negative taxable income and those with carryover losses, leaving them often with no taxable income to offset. For those users, the rental payments charged by a lessor, who is taking ownership tax benefits into account in setting its lease rate, can conceivably be worth more through the lower rent payments than the ownership tax benefits, which cannot be used, or can only be partially used.

The Importance of Lease Structuring

When the lessor anticipates tax benefits as a profit component, they will likely suffer an economic loss if those benefits are unavailable. Those benefits will be available only if the lessor remains the equipment owner for tax purposes. And, the lessor will be treated as the tax owner only if the lease is a true lease for tax purposes. To qualify as a true lease for tax purposes, certain tax guidelines must be met, as explained in Chapter 5.

Poor lease structuring can lead to disaster for both the lessee and the lessor. If the transaction does not qualify as a true lease for tax purposes, the lessee will not be able to deduct the rental payments and the lessor cannot use the ownership tax benefits. For example, if the lease was successfully classified by the Internal Revenue Service as a loan, the lessee would be deemed the equipment owner and the lessor deemed the lender. Then, if the lessee cannot use any tax benefits and the lessor must have them for the transaction to make economic sense, everyone loses.

> **Observation:** While all leases must be true leases for the lessor to obtain tax benefits, for leases where the lease term is significantly shorter than the equipment's useful life, the lessor has not amortized their equipment cost through rent payments over the lease term, and there is no fixed-price lessee equipment purchase option, there will be little risk that the lease will not be treated as a true lease, because the lessor's ownership status will be clear. Generally, the closer the lease term comes to matching the equipment's useful life to the lessee, the more attention that must be paid to the true lease tax rules.

The Pros and Cons of Leasing for a Business Lessee

Leasing is not always the best way for every user to acquire equipment. In some circumstances, it is advisable; in others, buying equipment is the right decision. Whether or not to lease certain equipment is not always an easy decision, and in each situation, the user must weigh all the advantages and disadvantages. This section will provide you with the basic considerations essential to making a comprehensive evaluation.

Advantages of Leasing

Possible Less Red Tape

Getting equipment financing from an independent leasing company can require less red tape and time than in arranging an equipment loan transaction with a bank. Because an independent leasing company's credit process may be less rigorous or substantially shorter, working with it can better ensure the necessary financing. And, the typical documentation time and expense that can be saved can offset an equipment lease interest rate that is higher than a loan interest rate. This is particularly true when the cost of the equipment involved is relatively small.

May Minimize Obsolescence Concerns

If you are concerned that equipment your company needs may become obsolete before the end of its useful life and, therefore, have little or no re-sale value, leasing can reduce that risk if the lessor assumes the obsolescence risk by basing part of its investment return on a significant end-of-lease equipment sale or re-lease value. The greater the residual value assumed by the lessor (thereby amortizing less of the equipment cost through rents), the less rent your company will pay over the lease term. Typically, high-tech equipment users, where new, more efficient models quickly outdate their predecessors, are faced with an obsolescence issue.

As a practical matter, as long as the equipment does its job, does it really matter whether there is better equipment available? In some situations, it does. For example, a more efficient item of manufacturing equipment may lower production costs by a sufficient amount so that a user may want to acquire a new model before the old model has been written off to insure its price-competitive position in the market. If a user had bought, rather than leased, the equipment, the overall cost of replacing it could be expensive. And, if the used equipment's market value was significantly less than its remaining financial reporting account *book* value at the time of replacement, the user would have what might be a potentially undesirable book loss in addition to the replacement cash outlay.

As any lessor also runs the risk of financial loss through equipment obsolescence, to protect themself, they will typically build a premium into its rate to compensate for the risk. A prospective lessee may be willing to pay the premium as a form of insurance against a loss through obsolescence. Of course, if the equipment does not become obsolete, the increased rental rate will have reduced the profits it could have made had it owned the equipment.

Recommendation: Because it is impossible to determine without question whether equipment will become obsolete, the obsolescence risk issue can be a real dilemma. However, by evaluating the past history of the type of equipment under consideration with, say, an equipment appraiser, you may be able to comfortably predict its obsolescence likelihood.

Ideal When There Are Limited Use Needs

When equipment is needed only for a limited period of time, leasing can be an effective way of acquiring its use, assuming your company can obtain the lease terms that fits its needs. Leasing equipment for the period it will be needed eliminates the re-marketing risks your company would have at the end of a short use period, and also permits a more defined estimate of the effective cost of using the equipment. For example, a public utility building its own plant often must acquire certain specialized construction equipment to do the job. Once the plant is finished, the equipment may be of no further use to the utility, but it may still have many years of useful life left. If it cannot be sold for a reasonable price, the overall cost of its use can be high. Leasing removes the resale risk and would allow the utility to determine in advance the total effective usage cost.

Preserves Capital

A key advantage to leasing for many equipment users is that it helps preserve their existing funds or bank lines of credit for other uses. The absence of a lease financing down payment, in effect 100 percent financing, can assist high growth rate companies in maximizing their use of funds. That can be particularly attractive in periods of tight money.

> **Recommendation:** When you are evaluating whether to lease or to buy equipment, you must carefully consider the real cost of borrowed funds, explained in greater detail in Chapter 7. For example, a high compensating balance requirement can easily increase your effective cost of a bank loan. When this type of collateral loan cost increases, the attractiveness of leasing usually increases.

Obtain Value-Added Technical or Administrative Services

Equipment users who lack the staff or expertise to handle specialized equipment needs can address this issue through a service lease, where those necessary technical or administrative services are provided along with the equipment. Additionally, service leases can assist users in avoiding tying up time and manpower in activities that are outside of their normal operations. There is, of course, generally a charge, built into the rent, for the nonfinancial services supplied. Typically, lessors of office equipment, trucks, automobiles, and railcars offer some form of non-financial services as a supplement to their financing. For example, railcar lessors frequently offer maintenance services.

A Way Around Certain Borrowing Problems

Users with credit or borrowing challenges may have an easier time getting leasing companies to finance their equipment needs because leasing companies often impose less stringent credit requirements than traditional lenders. Some leasing companies, particularly those with specialized equipment expertise, are generally willing to take greater credit risks because they are more able to deal with used equipment than traditional lenders can if they must take possession from a defaulting lessee. This is not to say that leasing companies will provide equipment financing to a user regardless of their financial condition. There still must be a reasonable assurance that the user will be able to meet the lease payments.

A Way to Trade Tax Benefits for Lower Rent

It is common for an equipment user to be unable to use the general equipment ownership tax benefits, basically depreciation deductions and, to a limited extent, any available investment tax credit. It may, for example, have an excess of accumulated tax benefits or insufficient earnings, due to poor performance or to major acquisitions, which have used up its tax bill. In this case, a company can indirectly take advantage of most of the ownership tax benefits through leasing from a tax-oriented lessor, one that takes into account in pricing its rental charge the equipment ownership tax benefits it has available; in effect, passing these benefits through in the form of a relatively lower rent.

> **Recommendation:** A tax-oriented lessor will not pass 100 percent of the equipment ownership tax benefits through to a lessee through a reduced rental charge but will make a profit on those benefits by adjusting the rent to reflect only a partial recognition.

So, it is always advisable to get several tax-oriented lessors to bid so that rates can be compared because the tax benefit pass-through in the rent may vary with each lessor depending on the value of the tax benefits to each.

Can Bypass Capital Budget Restrictions

Decisions to lease equipment are sometimes made to avoid a user's internal capital budget restrictions. For capital equipment purchases above a certain amount, a manager may be required to obtain prior *upper management* approval, and that approval may be difficult or impossible to obtain. If the equipment is leased, it may be able to account for the rental payments as an operating expense, even though the lease represents a long-term financing similar to a capital expenditure, to get around the approval problem. In this way, it may also be able to maximize its capital budget.

> **Observation:** Top management in an increasing number of companies have prescribed capital budget rules to avoid budget end-running, particularly with finance leases. For example, as long-term equipment leases can have a significant negative future impact on a company's earnings, particularly when cutbacks are necessary, very often, these transactions require senior management or, in large lease transactions, even board of director approval.

Inflation Hedge

Leasing equipment can provide a hedge against inflation. An equipment lease, in effect, gives the equipment user the ability to acquire equipment it needs at today's prices and, then, paying for it from tomorrow's earnings.

Possible Increased Cash Flow

Leasing equipment may be more cost-effective than purchasing it entirely with internal funds, or through the use of an equipment loan. Accordingly, the less the user has to pay to acquire necessary equipment, the more cash they have available—for example, their cash flow is increased. How an effective comparison should be made is discussed in Chapter 7.

Possible Off-Balance Sheet Benefit

Although no longer still a general leasing benefit, it is worth mentioning an old financial accounting and reporting advantage that may, to a limited extent, still be available in some equipment lease situations, discussed in greater detail in Chapter 8. In the early days of leasing, many users leased equipment, instead of taking out long-term loans to buy equipment, to avoid burdening their balance sheet with long-term debt liabilities. The lease, regardless of its duration, was basically treated in such a manner that its rent payments were deemed in their financial statements to be an operating expense. As a result, a company's profit to fixed asset ratios were improved that, in turn, generally permitted a greater bank borrowing capability. Today, the circumstances have changed. Regardless of whether significant leases obligations have to be recorded in the balance sheet or not, many sophisticated lenders factor them into their evaluation of a company's financial condition. But more importantly, today, the new accounting rules have generally effectively eliminated the traditional *off-balance sheet* benefit.

Financing Flexibility

The ability to obtain flexible financing is an important reason companies lease equipment. Your company, as a lessee, has the ability to have the terms and conditions of a lease arrangement structured to address your company's specific business needs. For example, lease arrangements can be set up with a variety of lessee options, such as fair market or fixed price equipment purchase options, fair market or fixed price lease term renewal options, early lease termination options, equipment upgrade options, and sublease options. Varying rent payment structures, such as low/high or high/low rent payments, and skipped rent payments during industry down cycles, as well as varying rent periodicity, such as payments monthly, quarterly, semi-annually, or annually, in advance or arrears can be negotiated. Master lease arrangements are available, which permit equipment delivered at varying times in the future to be simply added to an existing lease contract. And, leases can include services, such as equipment maintenance and repair.

Disadvantages of Leasing

Residual Upside Is Lost

When a user leases equipment, unless they have a favorable purchase option at lease end, they forgo the possibility of realizing a gain if the equipment appreciates in, or maintains good market, value during the lease term. Any such gain instead goes to the lessor. This can happen. For example, through inflation or buyer demand, a 20-year-old railcar may be worth more than it originally cost.

Many leases give lessees the option to buy the leased equipment at the lease term's end for its fair market value at that time. If the fair market value turns out to be high, the purchase price, coupled with the rent paid, results in a very expensive transaction. In such a situation, a lessee would undoubtedly have been better off if it had originally bought the equipment. The problem is that there is no way of telling what the future value is going to be, other than, possibly reviewing historical used equipment value trends or getting advice from an equipment appraiser, which still provides no guaranty.

There is, however, one way for a prospective lessee to limit its cost exposure if they believe it is likely they will want to buy the equipment at the end of the term and, also, share in any residual upside—a fixed price purchase option. Under this option, a lessee has the right to buy the equipment at the end of a lease at a fixed price, for, say, 25 percent of the original cost, something agreed to at the time the lease is entered into. If the equipment's market value at the lease term's end is high, say, 75 percent of cost, the lessee would have the ability to take advantage of the favorable market by buying it for 25 percent of cost and selling it for 75 percent of cost. There are, however, two problems with fixed-price purchase options. First, not all lessors are willing to grant them and give up their residual upside. Second, fixed-price purchase options can jeopardize a lease's true lease status for tax purposes if it is considered a bargain purchase option, as explained in Chapter 5.

Recommendation: If a prospective lessor is willing to grant your company a fixed price purchase right at, say, 35 percent of cost, you should request that it be at 35 percent of cost or the equipment's fair market value, whichever is less. This way, if the equipment's market value at the time of the option's exercise is lower than the fixed price, you will not have to pay more than the equipment is worth if a purchase is necessary.

Frequently, a prospective lessee's concern over the loss of residual value upside is more emotional than practical. The potential loss must always be kept in the proper economic perspective by, for example, bringing in a qualified appraiser to give an opinion as to what the equipment is likely to be worth in the future and discounting the value to its present worth.

Illustrative Example: *A Residual Perspective*

Company Able is considering whether to lease or buy a heavy-duty crane. Company Able's financial vice president recommends that it be leased; however, the operational vice president believes that it should be bought because of its favorable market value projection at the end of the period of use. The facts are as follows:

Crane cost...3 million U.S. dollars

Lease term...20 years

Depreciated book value at end of 20 years.............300,000 U.S. dollars

If the market value of the crane is estimated to be 500,000 U.S. dollars at the end of the lease term, Company Able would lose the chance at a 200,000 U.S. dollar upside gain ($500,000 – $300,00) if it leased the equipment.

What if, however, the potential loss is considered in terms of current dollars? The present value of such a loss 20 years out, computed using an annual discount rate of 10 percent, is approximately 30,000 U.S. dollars. Compared to the original cost of three million U.S. dollars and considering the fact that the upside gain may not materialize, the residual concern may be overstated, particularly if any down payment that would have been required if purchased with an equipment loan was put to productive use.

Equipment Control May Be Limited

When a lease ends, so does a lessee's right to use the equipment. This can create a problem for an equipment user if suitable replacement equipment is not readily available and the lessor refuses to re-lease or sell it to the lessee. While purchase or renewal options theoretically eliminate this risk, from a practical standpoint, when a third party owns the equipment, there is no guarantee it will abide by the terms of the options voluntarily. Also, there is always the possibility, although remote, that a lessor, or the lessor's creditors, will interfere with the lessee's right to use the equipment during the lease term, even though it may have no legal right to do so. Having the legal right of continued use may be of little consequence to a lessee when equipment essential to its continued operations becomes unavailable.

Key Situations When to Consider Leasing

In summary, there are certain key indicators that suggest that your company should seriously consider leasing:

- If your company must pay a high interest rate for money borrowed, leasing can be an economically attractive equipment financing alternative. Keep in mind, however, that equipment users whose credit dictates high borrowing interest rates may also dictate high leasing rates, because a lessor will offset any increased credit risk with increased lease returns. The cost of leasing, however, will probably not increase proportionately as high as the cost of borrowing.

- If your company cannot use a significant part or all of the equipment ownership tax benefits, you may come out ahead by leasing needed equipment. This, of course, assumes the tax benefits can be used by the leasing company, and the benefits are passed through in the form of a relatively lower rental rate.
- If the equipment involved has unusual service problems that cannot be handled by your company internally, for example, because of the technical nature of the equipment or your company's inadequate staffing, entering into an appropriate service lease may be the right decision.
- If implicit lease interest rates are about the same as debt interest rates and there are significant ancillary costs to borrowing, such as high compensating balances or commitment fees, leasing should be considered.

When a Lease Decision Is Warranted

An equipment user should lease the needed equipment when one or more of the following factors are present:

- There is a high risk that equipment will become obsolete before the end of its useful life.
- The equipment will be needed only for a short period.
- It is desirable to maximize available capital resources.
- Technical, administrative, or other nonfinancial equipment-related services that are not internally available can be easily secured from a leasing company.
- High interest rates must be paid for borrowed money.
- The tax benefits resulting from the equipment ownership cannot be used.
- The equipment will have a poor market value at the end of its term of use.

Checklist for a Prospective Lessees Approaching Potential Lessors

As the preliminary step in considering a lease transaction, an equipment user should address the following issues:

What basic type of lease arrangement or arrangements are you going to consider?

- Non-leveraged finance (Author's note: If you want a long-term lease and you need to get your lease in place in a hurry, this may be the best choice.)
    - (1) Net lease (Author's note: If you don't need the lessor to provide any equipment services, such as maintenance, a net lease is the lease of choice.)
- Leveraged finance (Author's note: This may provide the lowest long-term lease rate, but can take the longest to document because of third-party lender involvement.)
    - (1) Net lease (Author's note: See same category comment for the non-leveraged lease.)
- Operating lease (Author's note: This is the lease to use when you only want equipment for a short period of time.)
- Service lease (Author's note: This is the lease to use when you want lessor-supplied services, such as ongoing equipment maintenance.)

What potential sources of lease financing will be invited to submit lease quotations?

- Individuals (Author's note: A choice to use with caution.)
- Independent nonbank (Author's note: They should always be invited because they are often the most innovative.)
- Banks (Author's note: They typically offer fair lease rates, but the lease interest rates may vary depending on their internal needs, and they can be very bureaucratic to deal with.)

- Captive leasing companies (Author's note: If your equipment supplier has one, ask its captive lessor to bid on your lease transaction. Although they have the capability to offer the lowest lease rate, they often do not.)
- Lease brokers (Author's note: The experienced ones can bring solid value-added benefits to your lease situation. Know, however, who you are dealing with—some are not as ethical as they should be.)

If an individual is under consideration:
- Verify that the individual been involved in lease transactions before.
- Determine if the individual has experienced lease advisors and management representatives to assist him or her if transaction issues arise in the future.

If an independent nonbank leasing company is under consideration:
- Does it have a good reputation in the financial community?
- Have other existing lessees been contacted to determine how difficult it may be to deal with?
- Is its financial condition sufficient to ensure adequate and timely funding?
- Will the equipment be funded entirely from the lessor's own finds?
- If equipment-related nonfinancial services will be supplied, does it have an adequate staff and facilities to supply these services on a timely basis?
- How tough is the lessor's lease documentation? (A form of the lessor's lease should be reviewed before granting any lease award.)

If a prospective lessee's regular bank will be involved, will the lease restrict its future loan availability?
If a lease broker is under consideration:
- How many similar transactions have they completed in the last three years?

- What do other companies that have used their service say about their method of operation and their ability to follow through on a proposed transaction?
- Are there any banks or other prospective lessor-investors who should not be approached by the broker?

Summary

The concept of leasing equipment is simple; a lessor buys equipment and leases it to the lessee for an agreed-upon period. The economic and business decisions, however, on the lessee's part are not simple. There are many factors that must be understood and assessed before engaging in a lease transactions, including tax, accounting, financial, business, and legal considerations. Most important for the lessor is a lessee's credit worthiness and how much money they can make by entering into a lease. For the prospective lessee, the most important aspect in their decision is determining whether leasing, as opposed to buying, equipment is an economically attractive alternative. And, this cannot effectively be done without understanding what types of lease arrangements are available and who are the best lessors to use for a given situation.

CHAPTER 2

Understanding How the Equipment Leasing and Financing Business Operates

Overview

If you understand how someone you are negotiating with operates, you will have better negotiating leverage. And, that is the purpose of this chapter, to provide you with a general understanding of how the equipment financing business operates in the United States by giving you an overview of the key business elements of the leasing of equipment.

The Business Environment

The equipment financing business in the United States is mature, and competition is intense, and, accordingly, the traditional equipment financing business is not one easily entered by new companies. Mistakes are easy to make, particularly in the case of credit decisions. Something attested to over and over during the past decades by the many non-bank, and bank-affiliated, leasing company problems, closings, sell-offs, and bankruptcies from a variety of historically repetitive and obvious mistakes. Ones often the result of top management's lack of streetwise business and operational expertise, short-sighted attempts to maintain near-term profits, risky product financings, or the desire to increase profit-based bonuses.

Key Traditional Profit Strategies

Typically, there is nothing unique from a leasing company to another leasing company in developing and pursuing basic profit strategies. There are very few, if any, profit strategy nuances from one leasing company to another. And, once you understand how they make money, you are better able to assess your negotiating position and what you need to watch out for when dealing with a leasing company. So, understanding how these companies generally make money is essential. Aside from financing profits, there can be other profit areas, many of which are not obvious to a layperson.

Valuable Assets Acquired with Customer Money

In very simple, everyday terms, how would you react if a wealthy neighbor asked you to lease her an 80,000 U.S. dollars BMW for her business use? Assume also that the lease would be for seven years, the rents would pay off any bank loan you used to pay for the BMW and provide a 200 U.S. dollars per month profit and, when the lease ended, your neighbor would have to return the car to you in excellent condition. The result: at the end of seven years, you would own what could be a cream-puff BMW, free and clear, to do with as you wish. Sell it. Re-lease it. Or, simply use it as your personal car. Sounds good? Most people would agree that it does. That is the basic business of equipment leasing in a nutshell.

Now, let us take this hypothetical example a step further. What if 10 individuals asked you to lease them BMWs under the same terms that also provided you with a 200 U.S. dollars per month profit on each car? Your profit would be 2,000 U.S. dollars a month, and you would own 10 BMWs at the end of their respective seven-year lease terms, all free and clear. Not a bad return.

While this over-simplified hypothetical may not be realistic in the automobile financing market, an extremely competitive market where finance companies have to maintain an equity, or end-of-lease *residual* investment in a car making it unlikely that you, as suggested in the hypothetical, would have your entire investment returned at the end of the lease term with a profit, it does put into quick perspective one basic strategy used in the leasing business, getting credit-worthy companies to pay for, and maintain, assets that can be sold or re-released at the end of the financing term for additional profit, all the while making a profit waiting for their return. All the leasing company must do, once a lease deal is put in place, is to send out the rent bill, and deposit the payment checks when they come in.

Windfall Profits: A Possibility

Now, let us assume in the prior section example that, at the end of the seven-year lease, each BMW was worth 25 percent of the original cost and the rents paid off the entire BMW purchase costs. In addition to a 200 U.S. dollars monthly profit, selling each car at the end of lease would bring in 20,000 U.S. dollars in end-of-lease, or residual, revenues.

The residual value revenue expectations, what assets are expected to be worth at the end of their lease periods, are an important part of today's leasing business. It is not unusual for equipment residual values to range from 10 to 100 percent of the equipment's original cost—and sometimes even higher. The residual values, of course, depend on the type of asset, its return condition, its useful life, inflation, and market demand. For example, in the past, some 10-year-old river barges were sold for prices in excess of their original purchase prices.

In the early years of the leasing business, when competition was not intense and lessee customers were less sophisticated, financing rates (and financing profits) were high; what an asset was expected to be worth at the end of its lease term was almost irrelevant. A lessor had made all the money they needed from the lease transaction even if the asset had to be junked. But, as time went on, many leasing companies quickly found there was a lot of added profit potential in the sales and re-leasing of assets that came off lease. In fact, in the early years of the leasing business, many aircraft lessors made lottery-like windfall profits from selling off their end-of-lease aircraft, with some aircraft end-of-lease sale values approaching, or exceeding, the original cost. Add to that the fact that these aircraft lessors had returned, through lease term rents, all but a minimal amount (often between 10 and 15 percent of the original cost) of their invested principal, and made a tidy profit, and you had some very happy aircraft lessors. The same became true for lessors of other long-life assets. As you might expect, all leasing companies soon caught on to the aircraft and barge residual *end game* and began to stay alert for high residual return possibilities in other types of equipment as well. And, equipment residuals became such a major profit component that some lessors even adopted a strategy of acquiring multi million-dollar high residual value potential equipment solely for the end-of-lease sale or re-lease profits. They cut their lease term profits to the bare minimum necessary to win business, with rents often covering little more than basic transaction cost of money and overhead costs, anticipating substantial profits when the equipment came off lease. In fact, some leasing companies became so aggressive that they wrote leases that produced a loss during the lease term, counting on the possibility that after the initial lease term, the cash flow squeeze was over and yearly residual profits would provide solid bottom-line returns. Heavy reliance on residual profits is still one of the primary profit objectives in leasing today, particularly in *big-ticket* leases of long-life assets.

There is risk, however, in placing a primary emphasis on residual profit expectations. Lessors do incur the possibility that the equipment at lease end will not be worth much more than scrap value if there is no market demand for it or it becomes technologically obsolete. If rents just pay overhead, the potential for loss is great, particularly if unexpected costs are incurred. And, if residual revenue expectations are not met, there is little, or no, economic return for the effort. Some aircraft lessors, for instance, encountering a used aircraft market demand lull in the 1980s, had to store their off-lease aircraft and wait years for better sale or re-leasing opportunities. Today, equipment and customer industry diversification is used by lessors to reduce this type of risk.

The Customer Business Annuity

Developing an extensive customer lease and financing portfolio contact base is often a strategic business objective of every third-party and bank leasing company, something all learned early in the leasing business. Qualified prospects are valuable; customers who lease or finance, often lease or finance equipment again—at times, not even getting competitive bids. And, non-competitive bid situations can assure leasing companies of solid economic returns.

Additionally, with qualified leasing customer contacts, a leasing company has the increased possibility of readily originating new business with little expense—often a simple letter offering lease financing on new equipment acquisitions, with a follow-up telephone call, is enough to identify upcoming financing opportunities. Doing business with a good-paying existing customer has far less credit risk than dealing with a new, unknown customer. No matter how extensive credit due diligence is, it may not uncover credit potholes; financial statements and discussions with trade references and lenders, for example, rarely always tell the whole credit story. Clearly, there is no substitute for first-hand payment experience.

The Master Contract Strategy of Tying Up Repeat Customers

When dealing with new financing customers, third-party leasing companies have learned that putting a master lease or financing agreement in place pays dividends. Under a master financing arrangement, a customer can finance the acquisition of needed products through a simple addendum, cutting financing time and costs for all parties. As explained in Chapter 9, a master lease or master financing contract is a two-part document—the boilerplate portion containing the basic lease or other financing terms and conditions, which will remain the same from deal to deal, and an attachment, often called a schedule, which is a short (typically one to two pages in length) document that permits future business to be simply added by specifically incorporating the new product and financing payment terms under the provisions of the existing master, or boilerplate, document portion. Having only to review a one- or two-page document for lease or other financing deals allows future financings to be handled with minimal effort and expense on both sides. Financing companies with master financing contracts in place are often given a preference over competitors that do not because of the ease of documentation, in many situations, getting the last opportunity to win the business by matching the lowest bidder. In fact, in some cases, customers select an incumbent financing company even when it is not the lowest rate simply because the documentation does not need to be reviewed, making the documentation easy and the document review cost low.

Making Money in the Financing Business

There are many ways to profit in a lease or other financing transactions, some of which have already been suggested. The obvious areas for leasing profits are equipment ownership tax benefits and, as suggested earlier, interest charges and end-of-lease equipment sales or re-leases. The less obvious ones are interim rent charges, penalties for early prepayment, casualty occurrence payments, insurance cost markups, product upgrade financing charges, documentation fees, filing fees, maintenance charges, repair costs, excess use charges, late payment and other collection charges, and equipment re-delivery charges. The same is true for non-lease, or loan, financing, but the financing company does not have available the equipment ownership tax benefits and end-of-financing term re-sale or re-lease profit components.

The intent of the following discussion of leasing and financing profit areas is to simply identify for you all key money-making aspects so that you know where in your lease transaction there might be items you can negotiate.

The Basic Financing Profit Areas

The principal lease transaction profit areas are interest charges, equipment tax benefits, and end-of-lease equipment re-leasing or re-sale (residual) earnings). Not maximizing any one can significantly reduce the potential for transaction profits. As also stated earlier, for a conditional sale or other loan type financing, a financing operation would not have available any equipment tax benefits or end-of-contract equipment residual earnings.

Interest Charges

The most obvious way to make money in an equipment financing transaction is through financing profits. Financing profit, sometimes referred to as financing spread, is the difference between a financing company's cost of money and its overhead and the lease or other financing interest rate charged. The higher the interest rate charged, the greater the financing profit. For example, assume a lessor sets their base cost rate at 9 percent per annum, which included their cost of funds, and their allocated overhead, and charged a lease interest rate of 11 percent. Their financing spread is 2 percent per annum. By increasing the lease interest rate to 12 percent, their financing profit increases to 3 percent.

Market competition, reasonableness and, sometimes, state usury laws, even for commercial customers, limit how much financing spread a financing company can build into its lease or financing rate. Typically, the smaller the equipment lease or financing dollar size, the higher the financing interest rate that can be charged, with customers often looking only to the monthly payment amount, not the implicit financing, or interest, rate charged. For example, lease rates on 5,000 to 50,000 U.S. dollar equipment transactions at the time of this writing can typically range from 10 to 24 percent per annum, depending on the financing term and dollar amount involved. As transactions approach 100,000 U.S. dollars and over, financing rates move lower, generally in the 5 to 9+ percent range. Once the deal size hits 1,000,000 U.S. dollars, apparent lease rates can run 2 to 4 percent below the lessee's equivalent long-term borrowing rate. In the latter case, for example, a 4,000,000 U.S. dollar, 12-year aircraft lease for a lessee who borrows long-term money at 6 percent per annum could run anywhere from 1 to 4 percent per annum, or even less, depending on the equipment ownership tax benefits available and the end-of-lease residual value assumed (invested) by the leasing company. And, if the leasing company has an arrangement with a product vendor in which it can get a *blind product discount* (a discount that the customer is not aware of), the apparent lease rate can approach zero or even less, depending on deal structuring. A good example is in automobile leasing, where *0* percent financing is often offered, where the financing company affiliated with or owned by the car manufacturer provides an undisclosed car price discount in connection with the financing.

Equipment Tax Benefits

Very often, particularly in multimillion-dollar equipment leases, the tax benefits available to a lessor are a substantial component in computing anticipated transaction investment return, particularly when investment tax credits are available. In fact, companies with excellent credit considering multimillion-dollar lease transactions typically demand that lease rates reflect, and therefore, pass through to them in the form of relatively lower rent charges, at least a major portion of transaction tax benefits. The tax aspects of equipment leasing are explained in detail in Chapters 4 and 5.

Determining how to effectively take into account the transaction tax benefits is complex, but, fortunately today, there are many lessor profit (sometimes referred to as *yield*) analysis software programs, which make the job considerably much easier. One such widely used program, Super-TRUMP, is offered by Ivory Consulting Corporation of Walnut Creek, California (https://www.ivorycc.com/). The reader is referred to Chapter 7 for a discussion of the lessor yield analysis approach.

In the case of a lease transaction, the lessor, as equipment owner, has the right to claim the equipment ownership tax benefits, basically depreciation and any available investment tax credit. In addition, in the case of a leveraged lease transaction, the equipment cost of which is financed in part using third-party debt, there is another tax write-off available, the interest charges on the long-term equipment loan. In a lease situation, the lessee cannot claim for tax purposes of any equipment ownership tax benefits. It can, however, deduct the rent payments as a business expense. In the case of an equipment conditional sale arrangement, only the equipment user is entitled to claim the equipment ownership tax benefits.

End-of-Term Equipment Residual Earnings

In pricing a lease transaction (setting the lease rents), a lessor's ideal objective is to have sufficient lease term rents to return their entire equity investment, repay any equipment loans they have used to finance some of the equipment cost and provide a solid profit, with any end-of-lease equipment sale or re-lease (*residual*) earnings simply as windfall profits. In other words, setting the lessee lease rents using a zero-equipment residual value assumption. In small-ticket equipment transactions, this is typically possible. In a multimillion-dollar equipment lease transaction, largely due to market competition, this is typically not possible.

Additional Areas of Potential Lease Profit

A leasing and financing company can also add to its leasing and financing profits from less obvious transaction aspects, aforementioned, which include interim rent or financing charges, prepayment penalties, casualty occurrences, insurance cost markups, upgrade financing costs, documentation fees, filing fees, maintenance charges, repair costs, late payment charges, collection charges, deal re-write charges, and, in the case of a lease, excess use charges, re-marketing fees, and equipment re-delivery charges.

Interim Lease Rent

One way many lessors build in extra profits is providing for interim rent. Also called pre-commencement, or stub period, rent, it is the rent that is payable for a period running from the start of the lease to the beginning of its primary, or main, term. For example, a seven-year lease transaction might provide for the primary term to begin on the first day of the month. If the equipment is not delivered and accepted under the lease contract on the first day of a month, there will be an interim rent period running from the day it was accepted for lease to the first day of the following month. If equipment was delivered, for instance, on the 7th of January, the seven-year period would begin February 1, with an interim term running from January 7 through January 31. If the lease rents are computed based on the primary term rents, the stub period rent, typically a pro rata portion of the primary term rents, is a windfall profit. Although not typically found in an equipment loan-type financing, other than possibly a lease that is in effect a conditional sale arrangement (where there is a one U.S. dollar purchase option), it is possible to structure the arrangement to provide for an interim interest charge.

> **Recommendation:** Interim rent charges are often negotiable. So, before you make an award, make sure in the proposal (other considerations aside) the lessor waives any interim rent charge and starts the lease term on the date the equipment become subject to the lease.

Prepayment Penalties

A typical net finance lease may not be canceled for any reason—thus guaranteeing the lease profits, subject, of course, to a lease default. Some prospective lessees, however, want the right to terminate a lease early if the equipment become obsolete or surplus to their needs or simply for convenience and negotiate that right. The same may be true for equipment subject to a loan arrangement.

Generally, when a right to terminate a lease, or loan, early is granted, it is permitted only upon payment of an amount equal to a predetermined termination value, typically stated in a termination sched-ule. The termination payment is usually expressed as a percentage of equipment cost for each rent or loan payment period when a termination can be exercised. For example, a monthly lease might provide for a ter-mination payment of 85 percent of the equipment cost when the sixth rent payment is made, 83 percent of the equipment cost when the sev-enth rent payment is made, and so on. Properly structured, the payment of a lease termination value will return the entire remaining equipment cost investment, with the lessor's anticipated profits at least to the date of termination, and include funds to pay off any equipment purchase loans, any tax benefit recapture for taxes claimed but not fully vested, and add as additional profit an exercise penalty. A similar result, as applicable, can be obtained with a loan prepayment.

> **Recommendation:** The best time to address any early termination right is in the lease proposal, prior to an award. So, if this is a right you need, ask for it in your request-for-bids letter so that it is included in the lessor's proposal, allowing you to easily compare any termination exercise amounts provided from various lessors participating.

Casualty Occurrences

An equipment casualty occurrence, in effect, ends a lease. Typically, leases contain casualty loss provisions that require that the lessee pay a prede-termined casualty value payment. These payments are usually prescribed by formula in a lease provision or in a casualty payment schedule, often expressed as a percentage of equipment cost, all specified to be backed up by property damage insurance, which must be taken out by the lessee. Casualty value payments, like termination payments, are designed to make a lessor economically whole, including payment for any remaining unpaid invested funds as well as the loss of anticipated residual profits and tax ben-efits. For example, a monthly lease might provide, in the event of an equip-ment casualty occurrence during a specified rent payment period, for the payment of a casualty value amount equal to 98 percent of the equipment cost anytime during the second rent payment period, 96 percent of the equipment cost anytime during the third rent payment period, and so on.

In structuring an equipment casualty payment obligation, a lessor can build in additional profits to not only compensate for loss of its long-term investment opportunity, but to add more profit than planned through rents. When casualty payments are expressed as a percentage of equipment cost in a casualty payment schedule, one way they do this is to simply increase rock-bottom casualty loss payments by a percentage, say, 2–4 percent of equipment cost, added onto each specified casualty value percentage.

> **Recommendation:** As with termination values, the best time to address any stipulated loss value provisions is in the proposal, prior to an award. So, you should request that they be supplied in your request-for-bids letter so that they are included in the lessor proposal, allowing you to compare any stipulated loss values from various lessors participating.

Insurance Cost Markups

Equipment insurance is a must in any equipment lease or loan, and, generally, the lessee, or borrower, is required to provide the specified coverage through their insurance carrier. Although care must be taken by a lessor not to run afoul of any insurance regulations, providing the insurance itself, and passing the cost on to the lessee or borrower, with a markup, can create another lease profit opportunity. For example, a lessor might charge 14 U.S. dollars a year for a 2,000 U.S. dollar casualty insurance policy costing eight U.S. dollars a year, making a six U.S. dollar profit. On a 20,000,000 U.S. dollar equipment portfolio, this means 60,000 U.S. dollars annually. A lessor with insurance volume purchasing power can often offer equipment lease insurance at a markup, while still possible providing rates equal to or lower than that available to most lessees or borrowers.

> **Recommendation:** Identify during your lease proposal negotiating process if the lessor can make available lease required insurance, and if so, ask the lessor for the cost for comparison against what your insurance company charges.

Upgrade Financing

Equipment upgrades, when a lessee or borrower adds to or modifies existing leased or financed equipment, can provide an opportunity to lessors for additional profit. If the upgrade is not readily removable or has no standalone value, generally the existing lessor, or lender, is the only one willing or able to finance it. In these situations, a lessee, or borrower, has two choices: to purchase the upgrade with their own funds, in which case, in a lease situation, the upgrade may belong to the lessor at the end of the lease, or agree to whatever lease or financing rate the lessor or lender offers. If, as is the case in many lease situations, the upgrade is deemed, under the terms of the lease, to become the property of the lessor because, for example, it becomes an integral part of the leased equipment and cannot be removed without damage to the existing equipment, paying a higher financing cost may still be more advisable than purchasing an upgrade, which automatically becomes the lessor's property.

> **Recommendation:** If you believe that the equipment your company wants to lease may require upgrades before the end of the lease term, be sure to have that addressed, including the upgrade financing and rate, in your lease proposal before accepting it.

Documentation and Filing Fees

Many finance customers, particularly those leasing or financing small-ticket items of equipment, such as small computer systems are asked to pay stated transaction processing, documentation preparation and security interest filing fees. Small financing transaction documentation fees generally run from 50 to 500 U.S. dollars per transaction. Security interest filing fees, such as state Uniform Commercial Code filing fees, are generally nominal, ranging from 15 to 25 U.S. dollars. The more fees a lessee or borrower pays, the less a lessor's or lender's profit erosion.

Equipment Maintenance and Repair Charges

Requiring a lessee to pay for all normal equipment upkeep, such as maintenance and repair costs, protects a lessor's investment by ensuring that the lessor's profit and collateral value are not eroded by unexpected maintenance and repair costs if the equipment is returned. Simply, shifting the full cost burden of equipment maintenance and repair to a lessee eliminates or substantially lessens any necessary re-sale or re-lease refurbishment expenses if the equipment is returned at lease term end. This is a common provision in net finance leases.

Excess Use Charges

The better the condition leased equipment is in when returned, the greater the potential for the highest possible end-of-lease sale or re-lease profits. Another way a lessor sometimes ensures the best possible return condition and ensures profits is to put use restrictions on the equipment, which, if exceeded, provide for penalty charges payable at the end of the lease, referred to as excess use charges. Automobile lessors typically have annual mileage limitations, which, if exceeded, require the lessee to pay additional rental charges to make up for potentially reduced end-of-lease sale or re-lease value. Leased aircrafts are also often subject to use restrictions in the form, for example, of remaining engine hours before the next required maintenance cycle or prescribing a maximum number of takeoff and landing cycles, which, if exceeded, impose added charges.

Re-Marketing Fees

Equipment re-marketing fees is another way for equipment lessors to increase lease profits. For example, a lease may require that the lessee pay a predetermined fee to the lessor if the lessee elects to terminate a lease early or decides not to renew the lease, and return the equipment at the end of the lease, to cover the lessor's cost to re-market (sell or re-lease) the equipment. These fees are in addition to any other charges that may be payable, such as termination penalties, or costs to repair equipment to the condition required under the lease agreement.

Recommendation: Re-marketing fees are typically negotiable and something, if there is a concern, you should address during your lease negotiations.

Late Payment Charges

Leases and other financing contracts always incorporate late payment charges. If, for example, rent is not paid when due, there will be a penalty charge added to the late payment. Lessees often tolerate penalties in excess of the actual time value of money cost. In fact, some late payment penalties are as high as 5 to 10 percent of the rent charge.

> **Recommendation:** High interest charges are typically negotiable and something, if there is a concern, you should address during your lease negotiations.

Collection Charges

Although not strictly a profit opportunity, requiring lessees or borrowers to pay for any cost of ensuring timely lease or loan payments, many lessors or lenders, particularly small-ticket lessors or lenders, require that lessees or borrowers pay telephone charges on collection calls, as well as other collection charges, which could include the cost of a collection agency. Leases or loan arrangements can also include charges incurred for attorney collection fees. Anything that reduces business operating costs is indirectly a lessor or lender profit item.

Redelivery Charges

Equipment re-delivery charges and return location are another area of lease profit opportunity. It is not unusual for a lessee to agree to return the leased equipment at the end of the lease to a lessor-designated return point, free of charge to the lessor. This enables a lessor selling or re-leasing the equipment to add a small profit amount by also charging the new user a delivery fee from the lessee's location of use. And, at times, some lessors get lessees to agree to pay for all such shipment charges, regardless of where in the world the equipment is shipped.

> **Recommendation:** Re-delivery charges and location are typically negotiable and something, if there is a concern, you should address during your lease negotiations.

Summary

There are many components in product financing arrangements that can add profits, ranging from financing rates to end-of-lease term sales and re-leasing. Understanding what they are will enable your company as a lessee to better negotiate your lease document.

CHAPTER 3

The Proposal Stage: Where Your Lease Deal Is Made

Overview

As you now know, there are a variety of ways to finance your acquisition of needed equipment. The challenge is how to get the best financing deal possible in today's market. And, the fact is that the only way to do that is to approach the market in an efficient and organized manner. Otherwise, there is no doubt you will pay too much and miss out on benefits you could have received.

This chapter provides you with guidelines on how to efficiently negotiate your equipment financing to get the best deal possible. The objective, during what is referred to as the *proposal stage*, is to enter into a comprehensive outline of the leasing or financing deal you want—through the use of a financing proposal letter. Before you make a lease award and when there are other interested lessors involved, you have your maximum negotiating leverage.

Getting the Best Lease or Financing Bids: The Request-for-Bids Letter

How can you get the best lease deal? Simply, by shopping the leasing market to determine what options are available. And, to do this effectively, you must secure a meaningful number of specific proposals from potential lessors and lease underwriters. There are a number of ways to do this, but the best way is to prepare and circulate a well thought out and comprehensively written request-for-bids letter, commonly referred to as a bid letter.

While preparing a bid letter can be somewhat time-consuming, it is an investment that will pay off. This type of letter will avoid time lost handling telephone calls or other inquiries from lessors and underwriters asking for additional information on, or clarification of, the requested deal's basic facts. Most importantly, it ensures that bid letter responses will be on a uniform and, thus, comparable, basis, making it easy to select the best offer. Nothing is more frustrating than receiving, say, five proposals, each with a different rental payment mode, such as quarterly, in advance; semi-annually, in arrears; semi-annually, in advance; monthly, in arrears; and monthly, in advance. Not only is valuable comparison assessment time lost, but there will be a risk that re-quotes will be necessary because making valid comparisons may be difficult and time-consuming.

Another advantage to using a bid letter is that it makes everyone concerned on the lessee-side focus on what they need or would like to obtain from the leasing transaction. Generally, if you do not request a particular benefit, it will not be offered.

A sample request-for-bids letter is included in the Appendix.

Key Elements in a Lease Request

What issues should be covered in a comprehensive request-for-bids letter? Because the bid letter's purpose is to yield meaningful proposals, it should address every subject necessary to make a comprehensive lease financing assessment. At a bare minimum, you should consider the following points in putting together your bid letter:

- The equipment type and the manufacturer
- The number of equipment units involved
- The equipment's aggregate and per unit cost
- When the equipment delivery is anticipated
- The lease type desired, that is, for example, a net financial lease, service lease, or conditional sale financing
- The lease term and any renewal periods desired
- The rental payment mode, that is, monthly, quarterly, semi-annually, or annually—in advance or in arrears

- The extent of any acceptable tax indemnifications
- Whether the equipment will be self-insured
- What during and end-of-lease options are required
- A request for appropriate casualty and termination values
- Identify who, if and as applicable, will have the responsibility for the transaction's fees and expenses
- Whether, if and as applicable, a favorable tax ruling is to be a prerequisite to lease documents execution
- Whether, if and as applicable, a favorable tax ruling will relieve any tax indemnification obligations assumed
- The deadline for the submission of lease quotations
- When the transaction will be awarded
- Whether underwriting bids are acceptable
- If underwriting proposals are permitted, must the bids be on a *firm* or may they be on a *best-efforts* basis
- Potential equity participants and lenders who may be unacceptable if the transaction is to be underwritten

These points are explained in the following sections in the context of describing the proposal letter. A lessee proposal stage checklist has been included later in this chapter.

Your Lease Deal: The Lease Proposal

After receiving and reviewing your request-for-bids letter, interested prospective lessors and any underwriters will make their proposal responding to the bid letter's terms. Their response should be written and will be in what is referred to as a proposal letter. The proposal letter is important for a number of reasons. First, the letter will be your first opportunity to make preliminary selections from the bid letter respondents. Second, after reviewing the proposal letters, you may find you want to request changes or additions, because the letters will form the focal point for making your award decision. And third, after you have final forms, and you accept one of the offers, the letter will become the basis for your deal documentation.

Do You Have a Deal?

After the proposal letter is signed by all parties, do you have a deal? Yes and no. While in a sense you have a contract, usually the offer, and sometimes the acceptance, are qualified. That is, conditions are imposed that must be satisfied once everyone has signed the lease proposal. So, the conditions then subject your deal to cancelation, either by the lessor or you, if any are not met. For example, the offer may be conditioned on items such as:

- Necessary governmental or regulatory approvals, licenses, or authorizations
- Favorable opinions of counsel
- The effective placement of the debt, in the case of a leveraged lease
- Acceptable financial covenants, such as a minimum debt-to-equity ratio
- Satisfactory audited financial statements
- Mutually satisfactory documentation
- Formal transaction approvals by the lessor and any of its lenders
- A minimum dollar participation of equity and debt participants if the transaction is underwritten
- The receipt of a detailed equipment list
- Favorable equipment appraisals justifying the equipment residual value

The *satisfactory documentation* condition gives everyone the most room to find justification to back out if they want to because unless the parties can reach agreement on each term and condition contained in the lease documents, they do not have to go through with the transaction. This condition leaves room for some wide-open discussions on issues not even anticipated in the proposal stage, such as whether the lessee should pay for the equipment's return to any location designated by the lessor.

While the accepted proposal letter is usually not legally enforceable because of any stated conditions to be performed, it is important that, for a number of reasons listed next, it must be comprehensive, detailed, and in writing.

- While the proposal may not be legally enforceable, the parties will typically make a significant effort to complete the deal once the proposal letter has been accepted.
- The proposal letter serves as the guideline and reminder for the parties and their lawyers when they draft the documents.
- While unlikely, it is possible that if a party unreasonably backs out of the deal after the proposal letter has been accepted, it might form the basis of a legal action, particularly if financial obligations have been incurred by the claiming party.

Thus, a comprehensive and formal proposal letter is beneficial to both parties and should be used for every transaction.

The Proposal Stage Is the Time to Negotiate

Because the major terms are decided and the lessor or lease underwriter is selected during the proposal stage, this is the time for you to negotiate your deal. At this point, as stated earlier, you have a considerable amount of negotiating leverage, particularly if more than one bidder is involved. One bidder's loss will not jeopardize the transaction, and the bidders know it. Thus, your time to press for the tough concessions is before awarding the transaction. At this time, prospective lessors are the most likely to concede points just to win the deal. Once the transaction has been awarded, a winning lessor is in a much stronger negotiating position merely because the other bidders are no longer involved.

Your negotiating position will also be improved when you have a lot of lead time between a lease award and equipment delivery. If problems develop after the award, there may still be time to go elsewhere for the financing. If you do not have any comfortable lead time, this is not possible, but if the prospective lessor starts to *get tough*, some balance can be put back into the negotiations by telling the prospective lessor that your company is considering buying rather than leasing the equipment.

From the potential lessor's perspective, the negotiating strategy in the bidding stage is the reverse—the faster it can get you to *sign off* on a proposal letter, the less likely that you will make a problem request. Once the lease documentation has begun, particularly if there are near-term equipment deliveries, the prospective lessor's negotiating position has improved, often simply because you, psychologically, may be more reluctant to start over with new potential lessors once the document negotiations have started.

Issues to Address in the Proposal Letter

Stated simply, the proposal letter should outline the lease or financing *deal*. The letter does not have to cover every detail, but it should set the framework for the overall lease or financing arrangement. To do this, however, you must know what points should be covered.

> **Recommendation:** If an important point comes up after you have accepted a proposal letter, but before the lease documentation has begun, consider amending the letter to include the point. This will help eliminate deal point *misunderstandings* from arising during documentation.

Typically, although an underwritten leveraged lease situation will be more complex than a non-underwritten transaction, both types of lease arrangements usually contain most of the same basic elements. By understanding the more complex transaction format, the others will fall into place and, thus, the following explanation will center on issues that should be addressed in an underwritten leveraged lease proposal.

What Is the Offer?

While all proposals will offer to provide equipment financing, proposals from different types of bidders will likely have different consequences to a prospective lessee. One type of proposal is a direct offer by a prospective lessor to lease the equipment to your company, and another is an offer by an underwriter to arrange the lease financing of the equipment for your company. In the latter case, the underwriter may or may not have a specific third-party lessor in mind. Even if they do, the name usually will not be disclosed in the proposal to protect their position as a broker. For example, the under-written proposal may state: *The lessor will be a trustee acting as owner trustee pursuant to an owner's trust for the benefit of one or more corporate investor.*

Recommendation: In an underwriting situation, you are in a better position if you do not make an award to a particular underwriter until the underwriter has disclosed the prospective lessor, with a contact name, and you have contacted someone with authority to represent the lessor to confirm its interest and any conditions that may apply. If there is going to be a problem, the time to find out is when the remaining bidders are still in the picture.

In a non-underwritten transaction, the prospective lessor will make an offer directly as principal to lease the equipment to your company. For example, the offer may state: *ABC Leasing Company will purchase and lease to XYZ Company the equipment designated in this proposal under the terms and conditions specified herein.*

There are also many types of offer combinations. For example, a direct lessor could offer to purchase and lease equipment using in part their own funds and in part funds from a nonrecourse loan, a simple form of leveraged lease. Or, an underwriter may offer to put together a leveraged lease using one or more lessor-investors and one or more third-party lenders. Another alternative is that the underwriter may propose to bring in a *single-source* investor to act as lessor, such as a regional bank, that would pay for the equipment entirely from its own funds.

For you, the choice among the different variations may be a trade-off between delivery and price. If you have a near-term equipment delivery, you are well advised to limit your consideration to a direct lessor transaction, because dealing with one party directly will lessen the risk that the financing cannot be done within the short timeframe. If there is plenty of time, the best approach, if the rate is the lowest available, may be to pursue a syndicated leveraged lease transaction, where lessor-investors and debt participants are brought together by a lease underwriter.

Is Any Underwritten Offer Best Efforts or Firm?

Typically, in their proposal, a lease underwriter will state whether the offer is made on a *best efforts* or on a *firm* basis. A best efforts proposal is nothing more than an offer to try to arrange the lease financing on the stated terms and conditions. There are no performance guarantees, and the underwriter is generally not liable to your company if they cannot perform.

> **Illustrative language:** *"Best efforts"commitment: ABC* Leasing Company proposes to use its best efforts to arrange an equipment lease according to the terms and conditions set forth in this proposal.

A firm underwriting bid is simply just that. The underwriter states that they can deliver the financing under the proposed terms and conditions.

> **Illustrative language:** *Firm commitment: ABC L*easing Company proposes to arrange on a firm commitment basis an equipment lease for XYZ Inc., according to the terms and conditions set forth in this proposal.

From your viewpoint, whether to go with a best efforts or firm offer is like the choice among bidders—a trade-off between delivery time and price. Underwriters will often offer a better price on a best efforts bid because that way, they avoid being obligated to something they may not be able to produce in the marketplace.

The best efforts offer, however, has a downside for you—time. If the underwriter cannot, after having been awarded the deal, rapidly find a lessor, then valuable documentation time is lost. In fact, if the underwriter takes an extended period to market the deal, the possibility becomes greater that no lessor will accept the deal. *Reason:* Prospective lessor-investors become suspicious when a transaction has been around the marketplace for a while and may refuse to consider it for that reason alone.

> **Recommendation:** If you have adequate lead time, a best efforts underwriting may be the best choice if it has the lowest offered rate. If the winning underwriter cannot perform quickly, you can move on to the underwriter in second place without creating a timing problem as long as your award contains a performance time limit.

As discussed previously, even an accepted firm offer may not be a binding agreement because of the various conditions, such as the satisfactory documentation of the lease arrangement. However, as a practical matter, firm offers are more likely to result in a completed transaction. For example, there are situations when an underwriter will firmly commit to do the transaction, even though they do not have a commitment from any lessor prospects and is agreeing to buy and lease the equipment themself if they cannot broker it. This type of arrangement can be risky for your company as a prospective lessee because if the underwriter cannot sell the deal, they may not want to go ahead itself and may seek an excuse to justify a way out. For example, offers conditioned on mutually satisfactory lease documentation can provide an underwriter with an opportunity to create a document *disagreement* and, thereby, a basis to refuse to go forward.

> **Recommendation:** You should carefully investigate the financial condition of any lease underwriter offering a firm underwriting bid. If the underwriter does not have the financial resources to stand behind the transaction in the event it cannot deliver a lessor-investor, the fact that the offer is firm may be worth nothing.

A Direct Offer Has Less Completion Risk

If the offer is made directly by a prospective lessor instead of an underwriter, the situation will be different. Because the prospective lessor will use their own money to fund the transaction, the chances of the lessor looking for an excuse to back out are greatly reduced.

> **Illustrative language—direct commitment:** ABC Leasing Company, as lessor, offers to purchase and lease to XYZ Inc. the equipment following described under the stated terms and conditions.

Carefully Review the Equipment Cost Commitment

The proposal letter should identify the total equipment cost to which the financing relates. Frequently, a prospective lessor will put a limit on, or *cap*, the amount of money they are willing to commit to a transaction. For example, they may agree to buy and lease an oil tanker at a cost not to exceed 40 million U.S. dollars. Without a cap, they run the risk that unexpected cost escalations will cause them to invest more than they are comfortable with. So, an unanticipated cost increase over any *cap* may give a prospective lessor, who no longer finds the transaction desirable, an excuse to back out.

> **Recommendation:** If you are entering into a lease covering future-delivered equipment, make sure the lessor's cost commitment is adequate. For example, will it cover any allowable manufacturer price escalations? If there is a problem with determining an exact price, a dollar cushion should be built into the estimate. A word of caution, however, if a fee has been imposed by the prospective lessor for the failure to use all the committed funds (commonly referred to as a non-utilization fee). You should be careful not to build in an excessive cushion because any such fee paid on the excess over the amount used will increase the effective cost of the financing.

Make Sure the Real Lessee Is Identified

While the proposal letter will identify the lessee responsible for the rent, sometimes, the *real* lessee is not accurately identified in a bid letter and, thus, in the lessor's proposal letter. For example, if your bid letter named XYZ Inc. as lessee, but in fact you intend to have a subsidiary be the lessee, there will be a problem. If the lessor's credit review and approval are based on XYZ Inc.'s financial strength and if the subsidiary is the lessee, the credit check on the parent will not be sufficient, and, if there is not enough time to make any necessary adjustments, the financing may be jeopardized. Getting a parent company's guarantee may be enough, but it may be difficult to obtain at the last minute.

Identify the Rent Payments and Any Rent Adjustments

The proposal should specify how often, how much, when, and for how long rent will be paid. For example, a five-year lease may provide for 20 consecutive level quarterly payments, in arrears, each payment to equal 3.000 percent of the equipment cost, beginning as of the start of the primary term.

When a leveraged lease is involved, the rent calculation becomes more complicated. The amount of rent that a lessor charges is, in part, determined by the third-party debt interest rate, which will likely not be known when the proposal is submitted because the debt will generally not be secured until after the proposal award. Thus, to calculate the rent, the lease underwriter or lessor will use an assumed debt interest rate and calculate the rent accordingly. Then, to protect its return in case the actual interest rate increases over the assumed rate, a rental adjustment clause will be stated.

A rental adjustment clause enables the lessor using a leveraged lease structure to be protected against an increased interest rate, and a provision like the following is typically stated in the proposal letter.

Illustrative language—*Proposal rent adjustment: Les*see shall make 20 consecutive, level, quarterly payments, in arrears, each equal to 3.000 percent of the equipment cost, commencing on January 1, 20-. The rental percentage factor is based on the assumption that the interest rate on the leveraged debt will be 9.5 percent per annum. If the interest rate is other than 9.5 percent, the rental factor will be adjusted, upward or downward, accordingly so that the lessor's economic return shall be maintained.

Recommendations:

- You should precisely define the mechanics of determining any rent adjustment criteria, such as maintaining economic return, that a prospective lessor will use to make any rent adjustment so that the accuracy of the calculation can be independently confirmed. One solution is to have the lessor provide their computation methodology to an independent accounting firm that can verify the accuracy of any adjustment.
- Any time a rental adjustment is permitted, you should also provide for appropriate adjustments in values that relate to the rent, such as casualty and termination values, which verification you can provide for in the same manner as for any of the rent adjustment.

- If a prospective lessor has the right to protect their economic return by adjustments upward if the actual debt interest rate is higher than assumed because of a change in an index used when quoting the rent, such as prime rate, you should require, if not stated, a downward rent adjustment if the debt comes in, or the index is, lower than assumed.

Primary and Interim Lease Terms

The proposal letter must specify the equipment's primary (main) lease term and, if more than one item of equipment is to be leased, identify the lease term of each item.

Where numerous items of equipment are involved with deliveries scattered over a period, using an interim term in addition to the main or primary lease may simplify rental payment mechanics, but it will increase your effective cost of leasing, something you might want to estimate before consenting to a lengthy interim term arrangement.

> **Illustrative example:** *The interim technique for rent consolidation:* Company B wants to lease 120 trucks from Company A. The trucks will be delivered over a 12-month period at a rate of 10 trucks a month. Company B wants to pay the lease rent in quarterly, in arrears, payments. Company A proposes this solution:
>
> 1. There shall be four primary lease term start dates as follows:
>   a. First primary term: April 1, 20-
>   b. Second primary term: July 1, 20--
>   c. Third primary term: October 1, 20-
>   d. Fourth primary term: January 1, 20-
> 2. All trucks delivered and accepted for lease in the calendar quarter preceding the nearest primary term start date shall be on interim lease until the start date, at which time the primary term shall begin for such trucks.

Without the interim arrangement, both parties could end up with as many as 120 different primary lease term start dates and, thus, 120 different rental payment dates.

Structure of Owning Entity

In structuring a typical underwritten leveraged lease transaction, an underwriter may propose one of a number of different alternative entities to own the equipment, trust, partnership, or corporation. The underwriter's choice of entity should be decided and stated in the proposal.

> **Recommendation:** In a multiple lessor-investor situation, you should insist that there be a single representative with the authority to handle the lessor on the day-to-day issues to avoid time-consuming delays in getting the needed agreements to the changes required.

The Debt Arrangement

If a lessor proposes a leveraged lease, the debt arrangement and terms should be outlined in the proposal letter. Points to consider concerning the debt are:

- Who will find the debt?
- The debt repayment schedule
- The anticipated per annum interest charge
- The anticipated principal debt amount as a percentage of equipment cost
- The form of lender representative

While the proposal should cover these points, the lessor may need the ability to withdraw their offer, if the debt structure eventually obtained varies from that stated in the proposal, such as indicated in the following example clause.

> **Illustrative language:** *Debt structure:* ABC Leasing Company (ABC), or an investment banker acceptable to the lessee and to ABC, shall arrange for the private placement of a note (*indebtedness*) to be issued by the lessor for a principal amount of approximately 80 percent of the total cost of the equipment to certain

institutional investors (lenders). The lenders may be represented by an indenture trustee or agent bank.

This proposal assumes that the indebtedness shall be amortized in 20 payments of principal and interest at 9.5 percent per annum, payable quarterly, in arrears, over five years. The indebtedness shall be secured by a lease assignment and a security interest in the equipment, but otherwise shall be without recourse to the lessor. Any variance from the debt assumptions, other than interest rate, which is provided for in the rent adjustment clause, will relieve the offeror from their commitment thereunder, if so elected.

The proposal letter will also invariably state who will handle the debt placement and pay the placement fees. Typically, the underwriter or lessor will pay those costs. If the lessor places the debt themself, they will save the debt placement fee and, thereby increase their profit, but they may enlist the assistance of an investment banker. Keep in mind that, in particular, when the underwriter or lessor handles the debt placement, and there is a rent adjustment provision, it may have little incentive to make sure a truly rock-bottom interest rate has been found.

Recommendations:

- Where the prospective underwriter or lessor is arranging the debt, you should require the right to exclude any potential lender for a number of reasons. First, you want to protect yourself against a lessor obtaining an unreasonably high interest rate and passing it along through the rental adjustment clause. Second, you may not want any of your company's *line* banks to become involved because of potential future borrowing restrictions. And, some lenders are sometimes known to be difficult to deal with, and they should be brought in only as a last resort.
- You should have the right to disapprove any higher interest rate than assumed in the proposal to keep your lease rent within acceptable limits, no matter who places the debt.

Documentation suggestion: Many documents used in a leveraged transaction will be subject to lender approval. Some lenders can be difficult to negotiate with and slow in responding. To avoid last-minute problem delays, relevant papers should be sent to them as soon as possible and monitored carefully as to their review progress.

Tax or Business Reasons May Require a Narrow Equipment Delivery Timeframe

In some instances, the equipment's delivery date may significantly affect the economic benefits to the lessor. Most lessors will be taking depreciation deductions on the equipment, and when the equipment is placed in service determines the first-year deduction. Different dates can substantially affect the lessor's deduction. For example, a lessor may want the deduction in a current year because they have a substantial income to offset. Or, they may want it in its next tax year because they cannot use the tax benefits in the current year. Or, they may want it before or after its last quarter to avoid the mid-quarter depreciation convention treatment (see Chapter 4).

Business concerns can similarly dictate a narrow delivery time. For example, a lessor may not want to be obligated to provide lease financing at a particular fixed economic return beyond a certain date. Also, the prospective lessor may need to anticipate their periodic cash needs for funding equipment purchases. Future equipment deliveries can particularly be a problem when a long-term lease commitment involves many equipment items because of the likelihood of increased delays.

A solution to this problem for a lessor is to use a commitment period, with a funding cutoff date. This limits the lessor's obligation to fund to a designated period, six months for example, after the last expected delivery date. From your viewpoint, however, this may have a cost. The longer the commitment period, the more likely it is that a prospective lessor will impose a fee for holding the funds available. Such a fee, commonly referred to as a commitment fee, is usually based on a percentage of equipment cost. For example, a lessor may charge a fee equal to 0.5 percent of the total funds committed.

Recommendation: Any proposed commitment fee should be included in your cost-to-lease computation. A transaction with a lower rent and a commitment fee may be still be more attractive than one with a higher rent and no fee. Therefore, you should not automatically exclude a proposal just because it involves a commitment fee.

Equipment Location

The proposal letter should specify the location where you intend to use the leased equipment, something the lessor will also need to know. For example, if the equipment is used outside the United States, the lessor will generally have less attractive depreciation deductions and would lose any available investment tax credits.

Another consideration is that the equipment's location may have business benefits that affect a lease underwriter's marketing effort. Certain lessor-investors or lenders may be more willing to participate in situations involving equipment used in their local area. For example, if the equipment is to be used in Maryland by a division of a California corporation, Maryland regional banks may be interested because of the possibility of doing future business with a company they normally may not be involved with.

Purchase or Renewal Options

To have the option to continue to use the equipment as needed, you will want the right to buy the equipment, or renew the lease, under certain conditions at the primary lease term's end. To do that, you must have purchase and renewal options.

Illustrative language: *Purchase and renewal options:* At the end of the primary lease term, the lessee may do either of the following (with 180 days written notice prior to the end of such term):

1. Renew the lease for an additional year for the equipment for an amount equal to its then fair market rental value.
2. Purchase the equipment for a price equal to its then fair market value.

Recommendation: From your viewpoint, a purchase option should be exercisable not only at the end of the main lease term, but also at the end of each renewal term, with the renewal term rights also covering potential periods of extended use.

Right of First Refusal

An alternative to a purchase or renewal option is a lessee's *right of first refusal* option. Basically, a first refusal option gives a lessee the right to buy or renew the equipment under the same terms as offered to the lessor by an unrelated third party. This, however, will not give your company any assurance of equipment availability if you need it when the lease ends.

Illustrative language: *Right of first refusal:* At the end of the primary lease term, the lessee will have a right of first refusal as to any sale or re-lease of the equipment.

Observation: A right of first refusal can create a potential problem for your company as a lessee. It is conceivable that a competitor would bid for equipment essential to your operations merely to attempt to interfere with your business.

Early Termination Right

You may want what is called an early termination option, a right to end the lease prematurely as to any equipment that becomes obsolete or surplus to your company's needs. Some lessors do not like to grant termination options because they cut off future earnings. Thus, when granted, there is usually a substantial premium built in to exercise the option, referred to as a termination value payment.

Illustrative language: *Termination right:* At the expiration of each year during the primary lease term, the lessee shall have the right, at their option, to terminate the lease. The lessee will be required to give the lessor 90 days prior written notice of their intention to terminate and, during the period from giving notice until the termination date, the lessee shall use their best efforts to obtain bids from unaffiliated third parties for the equipment's purchase. On the termination date, the lessor shall sell the equipment for cash for the highest bid received. The total proceeds of such sale shall be retained by the lessor, and the lessee will pay to the lessor the difference, if any, by which the sale proceeds are less than the appropriate termination value indicated on the attached schedule.

Recommendation: If a prospective lessor is willing to grant your company a termination right, make sure that the termination values along with the right are incorporated into the lease proposal. These values are not standard and can vary significantly depending on competition and the lessors. Too many times, the values are not seen until after the award, and sometimes, only a few days before the anticipated lease document closing. If they turn out to be excessive, something you may not know without comparable values from another leasing company, it may be too late to go elsewhere for the financing.

Upgrade Financing Right

There may be situations in which your company will want the ability to have a lessor finance additions or changes, commonly referred to as upgrades, to equipment on lease with a lessor during the lease term. If the upgrade has no standalone value or utility, such as an internal modification to an existing computer system to enhance its performance, there would be only one lessor you can turn to for the financing—the incumbent lessor. If they are not willing to provide the financing, you only have two alternatives: to pay for the upgrade yourself, a cost that typically you cannot recover when you return the leased equipment, or to forgo the upgrade. To avoid this problem, negotiate an upgrade financing right, the basic terms of which should be included in the lease proposal, requiring the incumbent lessor to finance all equipment upgrades to their leased equipment during the lease term at a predetermined lease financing rate, or a rate that is to be determined by reference to a lending index, such as the prime lending rate, that will be fair to both parties.

Recommendation: If you are contemplating equipment upgrades, and require an upgrade financing right, the exact formula for determining the upgrade financing interest rate should be stated in the lease proposal and included in your lease. Doing so will avoid being forced into accepting an arbitrarily high rate offer from the incumbent lessor.

Equipment Damage or Loss

The proposal letter should identify a lessee's basic financial responsibilities in the event of a casualty loss. Typically, the lessor will require a lessee to pay a defined casualty value, which will allow a lessor to recoup, in whole, their investment. The casualty value amounts should be set out in the proposal letter so that they can be compared with all other offers you receive.

Recommendation: If you are required to insure equipment against casualty losses for the lessor's benefit, make sure any insurance proceeds received by the lessor will be credited against any casualty value payment that are due.

Tax Assumptions and Indemnification

A tax-oriented lessor generally anticipates receiving certain tax benefits, such as depreciation, as a result of owning the leased equipment, and, at least on middle-sized and large multimillion-dollar lease deals, incorporates the assumed tax benefits into the economics of their transaction. If the lessor does, those benefits become critical to the lessor's transaction economic return, in which case the prospective lessor's lease proposal will typically spell out exactly what tax benefits are expected, as well as any payment responsibility your company, as lessee, will have if the benefits are lost.

Because of the adverse economic impact, the loss of anticipated tax benefits can have for tax-oriented lessors, a prospective lessee is frequently asked to provide indemnifications against any loss of expected tax benefits. Lessees, for their part, will usually agree to some type of lessor indemnification against a tax loss, but will want to limit the circumstances triggering the indemnity as much as possible. While the precise terms of the indemnification will be negotiated during the lease documentation, what your company will be responsible for should be agreed upon in the proposal stage, that is, will you as lessee be responsible for any tax benefit loss for any reason, or only for changes in tax law or for losses caused by your company's acts or omissions? Clearly, it is best that you limit your company's tax indemnifications to losses resulting from your company's acts or omissions, something that should be stated out in the proposal letter.

> **Recommendation:** The particular parameters that will serve as a guide for any rent adjustment in the case of a tax benefit loss for which you will be responsible should be defined precisely to prevent a calculation disagreement. For example, at times, a lease will require the lessee to pay the lessor enough money, after taxes, so that their *net return is maintained. Net return,* or terms of a similar nature, can mean different things to different people. If there is no simple way to verify any payment adjustment in the case of a tax loss, you may pay more than necessary if the lessor tries to squeeze a little higher return. By the same token, you may incorrectly object to a legitimate adjustment. The best solution is to provide for an independent way to have the adjustment verified, such as agreeing to allow an outside, independent accounting firm to verify the adjustment.

Tax Rulings

In response to a taxpayer's request, the Internal Revenue Service (IRS) will rule on a transaction's tax consequences by delivering a tax letter ruling (see Chapter 5). Provided the taxpayer's request is complete and accurate, the IRS letter (called a private letter ruling) will be dispositive of the tax consequences. When a leasing transaction is particularly complex, or involves uncertain tax law issues, a lessor may require a private letter ruling on a transaction's tax consequences before entering into it. Or, if the lease is signed before a ruling in made, a lessor may agree to release a lessee from required indemnifications on issues addressed favorably in a requested ruling. If such a ruling is considered necessary, a prospective lessor will typically make that a condition of its proposal offer.

> **Illustrative language:** *The use of a private letter ruling:* The *lessor* plans to obtain a private IRS ruling with respect to the tax assumptions stated in this proposal letter. The lessee shall agree to indemnify the lessor for the tax assumptions that are the subject of the ruling request. Such indemnity shall remain in effect until a favorable ruling has been obtained on each of these points.

> **Recommendation:** Be careful about accepting a proposal where there is an IRS letter ruling requirement. The application and ruling process is time-consuming, and the actual ruling may take many months to obtain.

Transaction Expenses

The proposal letter should address who will pay what transaction expenses, particularly in deals involving an underwritten leveraged lease. When the lease is not to be an underwritten leveraged lease, the primary expense is legal fees, and the party incurring the expense usually pays for it. The matter is more complex in underwritten transactions, which can involve many parties—equity participants, lenders, trustees, and an underwriter—with resulting substantial expenses, such as:

- Fees and disbursements of special counsel for the lenders and their representative.
- Acceptance and annual fees of the lenders' representative (usually found in a trust arrangement).
- Special counsel fees and disbursements for the equity participants and their representative.
- Acceptance and annual fees of the equity participants' representative, usually found in a trust arrangement.
- Fees and disbursements related to the filing for a private letter ruling.
- Documentation expenses, such as reproduction expenses.
- Fees related to the placement of the debt.

In practice, the expense allocation is not as great a problem as it may appear because, very often, the underwriter will agree to pay substantially all the expenses. An underwriter may, however, cap these expenses by agreeing to pay only up to a specified percentage, usually around 0.75 to 1.25 percent of the equipment cost, and requiring the lessee to pay any excess. Because an underwriter makes their money by charging the lessor-investors a set fee for bringing them the transaction, the more they can limit their expense responsibility, the less they have to worry about fees and expenses eroding their profit. In a competitive market, however, many underwriters are willing, particularly if pushed a little, to assume the entire expense responsibility.

What If the Deal Collapses?

The difficult expense question is who must pay what expenses if a proposed underwritten transaction collapses. The lenders and the prospective lessor-investors will refuse to have any responsibility if the transaction does not go through, so that leaves the underwriter and the prospective lessee. Some underwriters attempt to put the responsibility for all expenses incurred in such a situation on the prospective lessee by inserting an appropriate clause in the proposal letter. Typically, the clause provides that the prospective lessee must pay all expenses if the transaction is not consummated for any reason whatsoever. This can be a dangerous position for your company as a prospective lessee, particularly when the underwriter's poor performance may be the reason the transaction failed.

> **Recommendation:** In a major underwritten lease financing, the expenses can be substantial. For example, it is not unheard of for the legal fees and other expenses in a complicated 10 million U.S. dollars leveraged lease financing to run anywhere from 200,000 to 400,000 U.S. dollars. Thus, you must carefully evaluate your potential expense exposure and clearly define the responsibilities in all events in the proposal letter, such as putting a cap on any expense responsibility you are willing to assume.

The Lease Type

As described in Chapter 1, there are a variety of different lease types, each imposing different responsibilities for the lessor and the lessee. Care must be taken to ensure that the equipment responsibilities have been clearly stated and understood, particularly cost responsibilities. A typical net finance lease requires the lessee to pay all fixed expenses relating to the equipment during the lease term, such as maintenance, insurance, and certain taxes. Without, for example, an understanding what the equipment-related expense obligations will be, your company's overall financing costs cannot be properly assessed. And, it can be an expensive surprise for you to discover after the equipment is on lease that your company must reimburse the lessor for a substantial sales tax the lessor owes.

Agreement to the Proposal Letter

Following any proposal letter negotiations, your acceptance of a proposal offer is simply done by acknowledging your company's willingness to proceed on the basis of the terms presented by your company's appropriate officer signing the acceptance directly on the proposal letter or in a separate writing properly referencing the proposal letter.

> **Recommendation:** Your company should *accept* a lease proposal directly on the proposal letter, not in a separate writing, particularly if the acceptance is conditioned. Separate papers can easily be lost or misplaced.

What Are Your Obligations After a Proposal Is Accepted

Because a proposal letter is generally a qualified contract obligation, as already stated, it may have no more than a psychological hold on the transaction because of various stated conditions, such as mutually satisfactory documentation. Thus, except for any obligation to pick up a collapsed transaction's expenses, your obligations may be minimal or nonexistent at the time of the proposal acceptance if the financing does not, in fact, go through as planned.

What Are the Prospective Lessor's Obligations After a Proposal Is Accepted

As stated earlier, because the lease proposal is likely conditioned, the offeror's obligations after you accept the proposal will also probably be limited. For example, if the offer is conditioned on acceptable documentation, as suggested earlier, a prospective lessor may also have no trouble finding *unacceptable* points and walking away from the transaction.

> **Recommendation:** If a proposal is conditioned on certain lessor credit or committee approvals, request that you receive written verification once the approvals have been given within a one- or two-week period.

A Proposal Stage Checklist for a Lessee

The following is a list of issues that your company, as a prospective lessee, must address during the proposal stage. You will want to review the list in preparing your requests-for-bid letters and then again when reviewing any proposal to make sure the necessary issues are comprehensively addressed in the proposal letter.

Equipment Description

- What type will be involved?
- Who is the manufacturer?
- What is the model?
- How many units will be involved?

Equipment Cost

- What is the total cost involved?
- What is the cost per item?
- Is the cost per item fixed?
  - (1) If not, what is the probable cost escalation?

Equipment Payment

- When must the equipment be paid for?
- Must the entire purchase price be paid at once?
- Is a progress payment necessary to the equipment vendor?

Equipment Delivery

- What is the anticipated delivery date?
- How long should the lease commitment run past the last anticipated delivery date?

Equipment Location

- Where will the equipment be located?
  - (1) At the lease inception
  - (2) During the lease term

Equipment Lease

- What type of lease is desired?

Lease Period

- How long must the lease term run?
- Will an interim lease period be acceptable?
  - (1) If so, what is the latest date on which the primary term can begin?
- How long a renewal period is desired?
- How will the renewal right be structured? For example, five one-year periods, one five-year period, and so on.

Rent Program

- When should the rent be payable?
  - (1) Annually
  - (2) Semi-annually
  - (3) Quarterly
  - (4) Monthly
- Should the payments be *in advance* or *in arrears*?

- If there is an interim lease period, how should the interim rent payment amount be determined?
  (1) Based on the primary rent (e.g., the daily equivalent of the primary rent)
  (2) Based on the long-term debt interest rate
  (3) Other
- If there will be a renewal period, how should the renewal rent be structured?
  (1) Fixed amount
  (2) Fair rental value

Options

- What type of equipment options are desired?
  (1) Fair market value purchase right
  (2) Fixed price purchase right
  (3) Fair market rental value renewal right
  (4) Fixed price renewal right
  (5) Right of first refusal
  (6) Termination right
  (7) Upgrade right
  (8) Other
- Is a right of first refusal specifically unacceptable?

Casualty and Termination Values

- If a termination right is required, will the termination values be a primary factor in the lease decision?
- Must the termination and casualty values be submitted at the time of the proposal?

Maintenance and Repair

- Who will have the equipment maintenance and repair obligations?

Tax Indemnifications

- What tax indemnifications will be acceptable, if any?

Insurance

- Is the right of self-insurance desired?

Taxes

- What taxes will be assumed?
  (1) Sales
  (2) Rental
  (3) Personal property
  (4) Other

Transaction Expenses (usually, only a concern in underwritten transactions)

- What expenses other than the lessee's legal fees, if any, will be assumed if the transaction is completed?*
  (1) Counsel fees for any lenders and their representative
  (2) Acceptance and annual fees of any lender's representative (trust arrangement)
  (3) Counsel fees for the lessor-investors and any representative
  (4) Acceptance and annual fees of any lessor-investor's representative (trust arrangement)
  (5) IRS private ruling letter fees
  (6) Documentation expenses
  (7) Debt placement fee
  (8) Other

- What expenses, if any, will be assumed if the transaction collapses?

Tax Ruling

- Is an IRS private letter ruling necessary or desirable?
- Can a favorable letter ruling be a prerequisite to any of lessor's obligations?
- Should a favorable private letter ruling relieve any tax indemnification obligations?

Submission Date

- What is the latest date on which the proposal can be submitted?
- On what date will the transaction be awarded?

Type of Proposals

- Is an underwritten transaction acceptable? If so:
    (1) Will *best efforts* or *firm* proposals be acceptable?
    (2) Is a leveraged or single-source transaction preferred or required?
- If "best efforts" proposals are acceptable, how long after the award will the underwriter have to firm up the prospective lessor-investors and any lenders?

Prospective Lessors—Underwritten Transaction

- Are any prospective lessors-investors or banks not to be approached?

Summary

Critical to getting the best possible lease arrangement for your company as a lessee is understanding what to ask for and how to evaluate what a lessor or lease underwriter is offering. This begins by putting together a clear and effective request-for-bids letter, one that gives the lessor enough information about a possible upcoming lease transaction. And then, making an informed assessment of any offer you receive from a lessor and any lease underwriter. During this stage, and before you make a lease award, you have the most negotiating leverage as a lessee, and you should use it to its fullest to get the best possible equipment financing available.

CHAPTER 4

Equipment Tax Attributes for Certain Leases

Introduction

A lessor's ability to write off, depreciate, the cost of the leased equipment can be a key income component in the profitability of an equipment lease transaction. Prior to 1986, another important equipment ownership tax benefit was available, a 10 percent equipment investment tax credit (ITC), eliminated completely by the 1986 Tax Reform Act (TRA), except for certain transition property. In recent years, however, an investment tax credit (ITC) up to 30 percent became available for limited types of equipment, such as wind and solar equipment, as well as fuel cells, often referred to as energy tax credits, which will at the time of this writing generally begin to wind down starting in 2020. The ITC does not merely reduce taxable income, but rather offsets, dollar-for-dollar, the equipment owner's federal income tax liability. So, a basic understanding of the applicable equipment ownership tax benefits is necessary to properly assess any tax indemnification provisions that your company as a lessee is obligated for under any lease. As a lessee, your company's equipment lease payments will be a tax-deductible expense for income tax purposes.

In the case of a conditional sale agreement or other equipment loan-type financing contract, the aforementioned equipment ownership tax benefits are available only to your company as the obligor of the financing transaction, because in those situations, your company is deemed, for tax purposes, to, be the equipment owner.

Investment Tax Credit: An Overview

Because an equipment investment tax credit, at the time of this writing, is not a generally available tax benefit except as stated earlier, a detailed discussion of how tax credits work is beyond the scope of this book. However, in the government's on-again, off-again pursuit of economic stimulus, because it is still possible that some form of general equipment tax credit, beyond the current available energy tax credits, will again reappear, a brief explanation is of use.

Basically, the purpose of tax credits is to encourage investment in new equipment to stimulate economic growth. The tax writers also used them to encourage the growth, development, and stabilization of a business area that the federal government seeks to promote, such as in the energy area.

An investment tax credit permits an equipment owner to offset their federal income tax liability by an amount equal to a specified percentage of the cost (technically, *basis*) of equipment acquired and placed in service in a tax year. Thus, for example, a taxpayer, including an equipment lessor, buying energy equipment in 2019 that cost one million U.S. dollars for which a 30 percent ITC is available could reduce its federal income tax liability by an amount equal to 300,000 U.S. dollars (30% × $1 million = $300,000) for 2019. It should be kept in mind that a lessor is only entitled to claim the equipment ownership tax benefits, such as the energy-related tax credits and available depreciation, for equipment under lease if the lease qualifies as a *true* lease for federal income tax purposes, discussed in Chapter 5.

Equipment Depreciation: An Overview

Assets owned, for example, by a leasing and financing company can be depreciated under rules stated in the Modified Accelerated Cost Recovery System (MACRS) in Section 168 of the 1986 TRA. Basically, depreciation allows the equipment owner to recoup their equipment investment over time, the depreciation period, and is an income tax deduction that the equipment owner can use to offset, as an expense, its gross taxable income.

Under MACRS, there are three depreciation methods, six recovery periods, and two averaging conventions that apply to equipment, depending on a variety of factors.

Property Eligible for MACRS

Besides meeting the MACRS requirements, to be depreciable, equipment must qualify under Internal Revenue Code (*IRC*) Section 167(a). Section 167 establishes the basic rule authorizing an equipment owner to a deduction, in computing federal income tax liability, for the exhaustion, wear and tear of property used in a trade or business or held for the production of income. All depreciation deductions under MACRS must fulfill the stated threshold requirements, that is, the property must be depreciable (subject to wearing out) and must be used in a business or income producing activity.

Generally, property qualifying under Section 167(a) may be depreciated under MACRS. Intangible property, property classified as public utility property (unless the taxpayer uses a normalization method of accounting), certain property that a lessor has elected to apply a depreciation method not expressed in terms of years (such as the unit of production method), motion picture films, video tapes, and sound recordings (such as music tapes), and property covered by MACRS anti-churning or transition rules are not eligible for MACRS depreciation. Additionally, certain other property must be depreciated under an alternative MACRS method, described later in this chapter.

How Are the MACRS Deductions Computed?

Four steps determine the annual MACRS depreciation deduction amount for any equipment. First, the total amount (*basis*) to be depreciated is determined; next, the applicable MACRS recovery class is selected; third, the appropriate depreciation method is applied; and, fourth, the applicable convention is incorporated.

Total Amount To Be Depreciated

The total amount an equipment owner can write off, and thus the annual deduction amount, depends on the owner's basis in the equipment. For MACRS purposes, basis is determined under general IRC rules for determining the gain or loss on the sale or other disposition of an asset and includes not only what the equipment owner paid for the equipment, but also the costs incurred in acquiring the equipment. However, an equipment owner must reduce the basis so calculated by any amount expensed under Section 179, discussed in the Expensing section following, by any amount claimed as a first-year bonus depreciation and, if a tax credit is available and claimed, such as an energy tax credit, to account for that credit. There is, however, no reduction for equipment salvage value.

MACRS Recovery Classes

The MACRS recovery class determines the period over which depreciation deductions can be taken. So, the equipment owner must determine if the equipment falls within the IRS stated 3-Year Property Class, 5-Year Property Class, 7-Year Property Class, 10-Year Property Class, 15-Year Property Class or 20-Year Property Class. For example, cars, light and heavy general-purpose trucks, computer and peripheral equipment, trailers and trailer-mounted containers are examples of types of equipment that come within the 5-year property class.

Depreciation Methods

Under MACRS, an equipment owner recovers the equipment's cost over the number of years in the recovery class plus one; for example, three-year property yields deductions over a four-year period. For equipment in the 3-, 5-, 7-, or 10-year class, a lessor generally uses the 200 percent declining balance method of depreciation, discussed as follows, with a switch to straight-line depreciation at the time that maximizes the deduction, taking into account the half-year or mid-quarter convention, also discussed next. For property in the 15- and 20-year classes, a lessor generally uses the 150 percent declining balance method with a switch to the straight-line method at a time that maximizes the deduction, considering the half-year or mid-quarter convention. Instead of the applicable declining balance method, a straight-line or alternative method of depreciation may be elected, discussed as follows.

Under the declining balance method, the equipment owner calculates the depreciation deduction for any year by multiplying the asset's basis, reduced by any prior years' depreciation deductions, by the declining balance rate, and then multiplying it by the percent available each year. Thus, for example, for an asset with a 100 U.S. dollar basis and a five-year recovery period, using the 200 percent declining balance method, the first year's depreciation is 40 U.S. dollars (ignoring the averaging conventions):

$$\$100 \text{ basis} \times 2 \times 20\% = \$40$$

For the second year, the MACRS deduction would be 24 U.S. dollars:

$$\$100 \text{ basis} - \$40 \text{ first-year deduction} = \$60$$

$$\$60 \times 2 \times 20\% = \$24$$

And so on, for three more years.

At the point when the declining balance method yields smaller deductions than straight line, the method switches to straight line. The 200 percent balance method resulted in more accelerated deductions than had been available under earlier depreciation rules. The IRS has calculated and published, in Revenue Procedure 87–57 [IRB 1987–42], the appropriate annual deductions applying the 200 and 150 percent methods for each MACRS recovery class.

As stated earlier, a lessor as the equipment owner can elect to use the straight-line depreciation method instead of the prescribed MACRS accelerated method established for MACRS property classes. Once an election is made, it is irrevocable (unless consented to by the IRS) and applies to all the MACRS-eligible property within the same asset class that is placed in service during the relevant tax year. The assets within the class for which a straight-line method is elected are to be written-off over the recovery period prescribed under the applicable regular recovery period.

MACRS *Averaging Conventions*

In calculating depreciation deductions, the handling of placements in, and retirements from, service that occur during the year must be addressed. Generally, under MACRS, a lessor recovers equipment costs using the half-year convention. Under that convention, equipment is deemed to have been placed in service at the mid-point of the year in which it was placed in service, regardless of when during the year it was placed in service. Similarly, an asset is deemed to have been disposed of, or retired from service, at the mid-point of the year during which it was disposed of or retired, regardless of when in fact it was disposed of or retired during the year. Thus, a lessor is entitled to one-half a full year's permitted depreciation in the year they place an eligible asset in service, and one-half a full year's depreciation in the year they dispose of or retires the asset from service. However, if more that 40 percent of the aggregate basis (essentially, cost) of property placed in service during a taxable year is placed in service during the last three months of that year, the mid-quarter convention applies. Under this convention, the first-year depreciation for all MACRS properties (with a few exceptions, such as for nonresidential real property) placed in service during the tax year is computed based on the number of quarters that the property was in service, with property placed in service anytime during a quarter being treated as having been placed in service at the mid-point of the quarter.

The Alternative MACRS Depreciation Method

An alternative depreciation system (ADS) must be used in certain select cases, discussed as follows, but can be elected in other situations. Under ADS, a taxpayer generally computes their permitted depreciation allowance by applying the straight-line method, without making a basis reduction for salvage value, over a recovery period typically longer than that specified under the other MACRS approaches. The applicable averaging conventions—the half-year or mid-quarter convention—apply in the same situations as under the regular MACRS.

When Must ADS Be Used?

A taxpayer must use ADS to depreciate equipment used predominantly outside the United States, that is, when it is located for more than 50 percent of the time during a tax year outside the United States. ADS must also be used for tax-exempt bond financed property, basically property financed out of the proceeds of tax-exempt bonds, tax-exempt use property, such as equipment leased to a tax-exempt entity, and equipment generally produced or manufactured in a foreign country.

When Can ADS Be Elected?

A taxpayer can elect to use ADS for any MACRS property for any MACRS-eligible tax year, but the election is irrevocable and applies to all properties in the class that the taxpayer has placed in service during the election year.

ADS Recovery Periods

Under ADS, a taxpayer will generally depreciate the equipment over the ADR class life period as stated in Revenue Procedure 87–56. The class life period is five years, for example, for automobiles, light general-purpose trucks, and qualified technological equipment.

Depreciation Recapture

Generally, on the disposition of MACRS equipment, the taxpayer must recapture, as ordinary income, the MACRS deduction, including any Section 179 deduction (discussed next), up to the amount realized on the equipment disposition.

Expensing

Under Section 179, an equipment owner can elect to deduct (expense) currently up to 1,000,000 U.S. dollars of MACRS property (excluding some types of property, such as property used predominately outside of the United States) used in the active conduct of its business in a tax year (the 1,000,000 U.S. dollar limit is the total per taxpayer, not for each equipment item). For tax years starting after 2018, these limitations are subject to adjustment for inflation. Additionally, there are other technical requirements that may come into play, so Section 179 must be reviewed in its entirety before making the election.

Summary

There are two key tax benefits that an equipment owner has available: equipment depreciation and, currently for certain energy property, an energy tax credit for new equipment. Each tax benefit in effect adds to the profitability of a lease investment for a lessor through tax offsets available.

CHAPTER 5

Understanding the Tax *"True"* Lease Rules

The True Lease

If the tax attributes discussed in Chapter 4 for a lease are important to a lessor, then it is important that the contract in fact qualify as a *true* lease for federal income tax purposes. And, if a lease qualifies as a true lease for tax purposes, your company, as the lessee, can deduct its lease payment as an expense for income tax purposes. If a lease does not qualify as a true lease for income tax purposes, your company is deemed to be the equipment owner for income tax purposes (and can claim the equipment ownership tax benefits); the lessor cannot claim the equipment ownership tax benefits and your company cannot deduct the lease payments as a rent expense.

Taking this another step further, if your company, as a lessee, is unable to timely use any available equipment ownership tax benefits, because, for example, it has a loss carry forward, entering into a lease arrangement with a lessor able to use the tax benefits and that passes them, at least in part, through to your company in the form of a favorable rent decrease, financing your company's equipment acquisition under a lease is a good equipment acquisition option.

What, then, characterizes a lease as a *true* lease for income tax purposes? The term is not specifically defined as such in the Internal Revenue Code or its underlying regulations. Two U.S. Supreme Court cases, however, established basic definitional rules—*Helvering v. F. & R. Lazarus & Co.*, 308 U.S. 252 (1939) and *Frank Lyon Company v. United States*, 435 U.S. 561 (1978). The *Helvering* case set down a substance over form rule—that the tax nature of what is purported to be a true lease depends on whether the lessor can be determined to have sufficient property ownership of the asset involved, taking into account all the surrounding facts and circumstances, to be accorded the tax attributes available to an asset owner, or whether the purported lessor is really a conditional seller, an option holder, a lender, or some other type of transaction participant. The case's decision was the basic guidance looked to until, in 1978, the advent of the *Frank Lyon* case, when the U.S. Supreme Court took another look at the leasing tax ownership issue and advanced in considering tax ownership, and therefor true lease status, that to determine if the lessor, rather than the lessee, is the equipment's tax owner, was whether the lessor had "significant and genuine attributes of the traditional lessor status," which attributes were in any particular case to be dependent on the facts.

While the ultimate *true* lease test is based on the transaction's facts and circumstances, the Internal Revenue Service (IRS), in 1975, provided guidelines for leveraged lease transactions (transactions financed in part with third-party debt), which, if followed, will help assure the true lease nature. In the form of four published revenue procedures (Revenue Procedure 75-21, Revenue Procedure 75-28, Revenue Procedure 76-30, and Revenue Procedure 79-48), collectively called the *Guidelines,* the IRS set out the formal criteria that must be met if the parties to a transaction want to obtain a ruling (referred to as a private letter ruling) from the IRS that the transaction qualifies as a lease for federal income tax purposes. Revenue Procedure 75–12, which contained the *foundation* rules for obtaining a favorable opinion from the IRS that a transaction would qualify as a *true* lease for federal income tax purposes, was refined and reissued by a later revenue procedure, Revenue Procedure 2001–28, which, together with Revenue Procedure 2001–29, now comprises what are referred to as the *Guidelines.* While nominally limited to ruling requests (when the IRS is formally asked for an opinion), the *Guidelines* provide helpful guidance on achieving true lease status even where the parties to the transaction do not request an IRS private letter ruling and even if the lease is not a leveraged lease, where the lessor borrows a portion of the cost of the equipment from a third-party lender. Additionally, industry practice is that even if a lease is not a leveraged lease, to the extent that the *Guidelines* may apply, they are generally followed.

Prior to the issuance of the *Guidelines*, the parities to a lease transaction found some guidance in Revenue Ruling 55–540 [1955–2 CB 39], discussed later in this chapter. Revenue Ruling 55–540, which still has guidance applicability, focuses primarily on describing aspects of a transaction that would cause it to fail to qualify as a true lease. It has applicability to *all* purported lease transactions, not just *leveraged* lease transactions.

Ensuring True Lease Treatment

How do the parties maximize their chances of obtaining true lease status? The best two alternatives—obtain an IRS private ruling letter or proceed without one while following the *Guidelines, as applicable,* and Revenue Ruling 55–540.

Getting an IRS Private Letter Ruling

As a general matter, if a taxpayer submits a ruling request to the IRS concerning a lease transaction, the IRS, after reviewing the request, will rule on some or all the transaction's tax consequences. Provided the information submitted is accurate and complete, if the transaction parties receive a favorable ruling from the IRS, they can be rest assured that the transaction's anticipated tax results will not be challenged. It should be noted, however, that even if all the *Guidelines* are not met, the IRS will still consider a favorable ruling that a transaction qualifies as a true lease in appropriate cases based on all the facts and circumstances. While the safest route is to obtain a ruling, it is typically not the optimum alternative for a number of reasons: preparing and submitting the request involves a significant amount of legal work, resulting in a higher transaction cost; a fee must be paid to the IRS, submitting a request takes a considerable amount of time (both to prepare the request and for the IRS to rule); and if the IRS's ruling is unfavorable and the transaction has been closed, there is a risk that this will draw attention to an issue that may otherwise have gone unnoticed.

Following the IRS Tax Lease Rules

When an IRS letter ruling is not practical, the next safest approach is to structure a lease transaction so that it complies with the IRS's *Guidelines* to the extent they apply, understanding the *Guidelines* were designed to address leases structured as leveraged leases. Although, the *Guidelines* do not establish as a matter a law whether a transaction will or will not qualify as a true lease, as a practical matter, it is highly unlikely that a transaction meeting the *Guidelines* would have IRS audit problems.

The IRS Tax Guidelines

As mentioned, Revenue Procedure 75–21, was modified and superseded by Revenue Procedure 2001–28. Revenue Procedure 2001–28 [CB 1156, 5/07/2001] generally sets out the conditions that must be met for there to be an advance ruling on a leveraged lease, and Revenue Procedure 2001–29 [CB 2001–1 1160] sets out information and representations required to be furnished by taxpayers in a leveraged leasing transaction advance ruling request.

It is important to keep in mind that even though the *Guidelines* apply only to leveraged leases, as stated earlier, the parties to a non-leveraged transaction are well advised to consider those portions of the *Guidelines*, discussed next, that apply to the transaction aspects. In addition to following the *Guidelines*, prospective lessors and lessees will want to comply with Revenue Ruling 55–540 [1955–2 CB 39], explained next, which gives some general guidance on all types of leasing transactions, leveraged and non-leveraged.

The *Guidelines*, summarized, are as follows:

Minimum Investment Requirement

Under the *Guidelines,* the lessor must initially make an unconditional equity investment, referred to as the *minimum investment*, in the equipment equal to at least 20 percent of its cost. This can be done in a variety of ways: with cash, with other consideration, or by assuming the obligation to buy the equipment. The unconditional nature requirement is to prevent the lessor from arranging to receive, either from the lessee or certain lessee-related parties, all or any part of their equity investment back once the equipment is put into service.

The lessor must also maintain this 20 percent *minimum investment* in the equipment during the lease term. The minimum investment test must also be met at the end of the lease term, that is, the lessor must show that the leased equipment's estimated fair market residual value is equal to at least 20 percent of its original cost, and that a reasonable estimate of the equipment's useful life at the end of the lease term is the longer of one year or 20 percent of the equipment's originally estimated useful life. This is usually validated by obtaining an appraisal of what the equipment will be valued at lease end.

Transaction Profit Requirement

The *Guidelines* provide that the lessor must make a profit on the transaction. Simply, the lessor must be able to show that the lease transaction makes economic sense without considering the tax benefits. Not only must a lessor anticipate a profit, but they must also demonstrate that the transaction will produce a positive cash flow that is *reasonable* in amount, that is, essentially, the rents and other required lessee payments must comfortably exceed the aggregate outflows.

No Lessee Investment

Generally, the lessee cannot invest in the equipment by providing funds necessary to buy, add to, modify, or improve the equipment.

The Lessee Cannot Be a Lender

Under the *Guidelines,* the lessee and members of the lessee group, such as affiliated companies, are specifically prohibited from lending funds to the lessor to assist in the equipment financing. Thus, direct loans and other credit-extending techniques like that described in the previous subsection will transgress the *Guidelines* and prevent the issuance of a favorable private ruling on the transaction.

Certain Guarantees Cannot be Used

The lessee and certain lessee-associated parties, such as their parent company or sister subsidiary, cannot guarantee any equipment debt. Lessee-related parties, however, can guarantee the conventional obligations found in a net lease, such as rent, maintenance, or insurance premium obligations.

Any Lessee Purchase Option Must Be at Fair Market Value

To ensure that the lessee is not the equipment owner, the *Guidelines* prohibit any arrangement granting a lessee or lessee-related party the option to buy the leased equipment at a price below its fair market value. This rule essentially eliminates all low, or nominal, fixed price purchase options, such as one U.S. dollar purchase options.

The Lessor Cannot Have Right to Require an Equipment Sale

A lessor is specifically prohibited from having any initial right to require *any party* to buy the leased equipment for any reason, except when there are nonconformities with written supply, construction, or manufacture specifications, thus eliminating the so-called *put options*, an ability of the lessor to force an equipment sale at a predetermined price at the lease term's end to, for example, the lessee, a manufacturer, or an equipment dealer. For a lessor concerned about whether certain equipment will have any residual value at the end of the lease term, this is a risk they must assess.

Uneven Rents Must Meet Certain Tests

Step rentals, such as *low-high* or *high-low* rent structures, must meet certain guidelines. Uneven rents payments may be subject to Internal Revenue Code Section 467 and related regulations, with Internal Revenue Code section 1.467–3(c(4)) providing an uneven rent test, it being specifically stated in the *Guidelines* whether or not the uneven rent test is met will not affect a taxpayer's ability to obtain an advance ruling that a true lease exists. Section 467 provides for determining how uneven rents will be treated for federal income tax purposes.

Limited-Use Property

To obtain a favorable ruling, it is necessary to establish that it is commercially feasible for a party, not the lessee or a member of the lessee group, to lease or buy the property from the lessor, demonstrating that it is not limited-use property. Limited-use property is a property not expected to be useful to, or usable by, the lessor, except for purposes of continued leasing or transfer to the lessee or a member of the lessee group; so, in effect, if the property is limited-use property, the lessee will receive the equipment's ownership benefits for substantially its entire useful life.

What Must an IRS Private Letter Ruling Request Contain?

In submitting a ruling request to the IRS, the taxpayer must present the information the *Guidelines* require in the manner prescribed by Revenue Procedure 2001–28, as modified by Revenue Procedure 2001–29. Generally, all the parties to the transaction, including the lessor and lessee, must join in the ruling request. The request must contain a summary of the surrounding facts. The request must be accompanied by certain relevant documents, such as the lease, any economic analysis, prospectus, or other document used to induce the lessor to invest (if the transaction was brokered, the type and quality of the leased equipment, whether the equipment is new, reconstructed, used, or rebuilt, when, how, and where the equipment will be, or was, first placed in service or use, whether the equipment will be permanently or temporarily attached to land, buildings, or other property, and the flow of funds among the parties). Additionally, the request must disclose the lease term and any renewals or extensions, and any purchase and sale options.

The Foundation Tax Rules

Two decades before issuing the initial *Guidelines,* the IRS issued Revenue Ruling 55–540 [1955–12 CB 39] detailing the factors that it considered in deciding whether a leasing transaction is really a conditional sale for tax purposes. Unlike the current *Guidelines,* Revenue Ruling 55–540 sets out the IRS audit position, rather than dealing with what is required to obtain a ruling. This ruling, however, is much less useful than the *Guidelines* because it is less precise. But, by checking its tests, you will help assure a leasing transaction's tax viability.

In this ruling, the IRS stated generally that whether an agreement, which in form is a lease, is in substance a conditional sales contract depends upon the intent of the parties as evidenced by the provisions of the agreement, read in the light of the facts and circumstances existing at the time the agreement was executed.

The IRS then went on to state that an intent that would cause an arrangement to be treated as a sale instead of a lease for tax purposes is found if one or more of the following factors exist:

- Portions of the periodic payments are specifically made applicable to an equity interest to be acquired by the lessee.
- The lessee will acquire title to the property under lease on the payment of a stated number of *rentals* that the lessee under the contract must make.
- The total amount that the lessee must pay for a relatively short period of use constitutes an inordinately large proportion of the total sum required to acquire title.
- The agreed *rental* payments materially exceed the current fair rental value.
- The property may be acquired by the lessee under a purchase option at a price that is nominal in relation to the property's value at the time the option may be exercised (determined at the time the agreement was entered into) or which is relatively small when compared to the total payments that the lessee must make.
- Some portion of the periodic payments is specifically designated as interest or is otherwise readily recognizable as the equivalent of interest.

It is interesting to note that Revenue Ruling 55–540 provides guidelines for determining whether a conditional sale contract exists. The assumption is that if a conditional sales contract does not exist and the parties structured the transaction as a tax lease, everyone is on safe ground. If the transaction is structurally complex, experienced tax-leasing counsel may be necessary to get adequate assurances.

Summary

If the parties to a lease transaction intend to have the lease characterized for tax purposes as a lease, they must know the tax rules governing whether a transaction will, in fact, be considered by the applicable taxing authorities as a *true* lease for tax purposes. If a lease is so considered, the lessor will be deemed to be the lease asset's owner and, thus, able to claim the available equipment ownership tax benefits. The lessee, on the other hand, will be entitled to deduct the lease rent payable as an expense of its income tax returns. Failure of the lease to so qualify can result in an unfortunate re-arranging of the tax attributes assumed to be available, with the potential of an economic loss for the lessor, and a less attractive arrangement for the lessee. To avoid this problem, the rules governing the tax characterization must be understood. Unfortunately, doing this is often an art, because the tax rules are not always precise or clearly discernable.

CHAPTER 6

Advantages and Risks of Leveraged Leasing Decisions

What Is the Concept of Leveraged Leasing?

The leveraged lease can be one of the most complex and sophisticated vehicles for financing capital equipment in today's financial marketplace. The individuals and firms in the leveraged leasing industry are aggressive and creative. As a result, the environment is one of innovation and intense competition.

Is the concept of a leveraged lease complex? Not really. It is simply a lease transaction in which the lessor puts in only a portion, usually 20 to 40 percent, of the funds necessary to buy the equipment and a third-party lender supplies the remainder. Because the benefits available to the lessor are generally based on the entire equipment cost, the lessor's investment is said to be *leveraged* with third-party debt.

Generally, the third-party loan is on a nonrecourse-to-the-lessor basis and ranges from 60 to 80 percent of the equipment's cost. The nonrecourse nature means the lender can only look to the lessee, the stream of rental payments that have been assigned to it, and the equipment for repayment. The lessor has no repayment responsibility to the lender even if the lessee defaults, and the loan becomes uncollectible.

The fact that a nonrecourse lender cannot look to the lessor for the loan repayment if there is a problem is not as bad as it seems for two reasons. The lender will not provide a nonrecourse loan unless the lessee is creditworthy and the lessor's rights to any proceeds come behind (are subordinated) to any proceeds coming from a sale or re-release of the equipment. So, if a lender only contributed, for example, 70 percent of the funds necessary, the subordination arrangement could put it in an over-collateralized loan position that, in turn, would decrease its lending risk.

Although the third-party loan is usually made on a nonrecourse basis, this is not always the case. If the lessee's financial condition is weak, a lender may only be willing to make a recourse loan under which they can look to, or has recourse against, the lessor for repayment if they cannot be satisfied through the lessee or the equipment. The lessor still, however, has the economic advantage of a leveraged investment.

Although the concept of leveraging a lease investment is simple, the mechanics of putting one together is often complex. Leveraged lease transactions, particularly ones involving major million-dollar commitments, frequently involve many parties brought together through intricate arrangements. The *lessor* is typically a group of investors joined together by a partnership or trust structure. The partnership or trust is the legal owner, or *titleholder*, of the equipment. The *lender* is often a group of lenders usually acting through a trust arrangement. This is further complicated by the fact that each participant will be represented by counsel with varying views. As a result, the job of organizing, drafting, and negotiating the necessary documents is generally very difficult.

> **Observation:** Because the expenses involved in documenting a leveraged lease can be substantial, typically transactions involving less than two million U.S. dollar worth of equipment can be economically difficult to structure as a leveraged lease. If, however, documentation fees (such as counsel fees) can be kept within reason, smaller equipment amounts can be financed in this manner. In many cases a prospective lessor or underwriter has an in-house legal staff with the ability to originate and negotiate the required documents. If so, this will help keep costs down.

Generally, leveraged lease financings are arranged for prospective lessees by companies or individuals who specialize in structuring and negotiating these types of leases. These individuals and firms are referred to as lease underwriters. Essentially, their function is to structure the lease economics, find the lessor-investors, and provide the necessary expertise to ensure that the transaction will get done. In a limited number of situations, they also find the debt participants. They do not generally participate as an investor in the equipment.

The premise on which lease underwriting services are provided by an underwriter (that is, on a *best efforts* or *firm* basis, discussed briefly earlier in this book) varies significantly. It is, therefore, worthwhile at this stage to explore the two types of underwriter offers: *best efforts* and *firm commitment* underwriting arrangements.

A Best Efforts *Underwriting Arrangement Can Be Risky*

Underwritten lease transactions are frequently bid on a *best efforts* basis. This is an offer by the underwriter to do the best they can to put a transaction together under the terms set out in their proposal letter. There are no guarantees of performance. As a result, your company, as a prospective lessee accepting the offer, may not know for some time whether you have the financing.

In practice, a best efforts underwriting is not as risky as it appears. Most reputable underwriters have a good feel for the market when bidding on this basis and usually can deliver what they propose. Thus, there is a good chance they will be able to get *firm commitments* from one or more prospective lessor-investors to participate on the basis offered.

Recommendations:

- You must always, before accepting a best effort underwriting proposal, give careful consideration to the experience and reputation of the proposing underwriter before awarding the transaction to them. An inability to perform as presented can result in the loss of valuable time.
- When there is adequate equipment delivery lead time, you may be inclined to award a transaction to an unknown underwriter who has submitted an unusually low bid. There is, however, risk. If the transaction is so underpriced that it cannot be sold in the *equity* market, it may meet resistance when it is reoffered on more attractive investor terms. This can happen merely because it has been seen, or *shopped,* too much. It is an unfortunate fact that when an investor is presented with a transaction that they know has been shopped,

even if the terms are favorable, they may refuse to consider it and, accordingly, you should not be too eager to accept a *low ball* best efforts bid, unless you have carefully considered the underwriter's ability to perform.

- You can control the risk of best efforts nonperformance by putting a time limit on the award, for example, by requiring the underwriter to come up with, or *circle,* interested parties within one week following the award and then securing formal commitments by the second week.

A Firm Commitment *Underwriting Arrangement Is Often the Best*

From a prospective lessee's viewpoint, a *firm commitment* underwriting proposal is generally the preferred type of offer. When an underwriter has *come in firm,* they are guaranteeing to put the proposed lease financing together. Typically, before an underwriter submits this type of proposal, they have solid commitments from lessor-investors to enter into the transaction on the terms presented. This, however, is not always the case. The underwriter's firm bid may only represent its willingness to be the lessor if it cannot find a third-party lessor.

Recommendations:

- If an underwriter proposing on a firm basis does not have *committed equity* at the time its proposal is submitted, you may be subject to certain risks. Unless the underwriter is financially strong, their firm commitment may be worthless if a third-party lessor cannot be found. So, you must always investigate whether an underwriter has lined up one or more lessor-investors and, if not, the underwriter's financial condition must be reviewed to determine, before making the award, whether they have the financial ability to stand behind it.
- Underwriters sometimes state they have firm *equity,* even though they have nothing more than a verbal indication from a prospective lessor-investor's contact that they will recom-

mend the transaction to their approving committee. So, you should always ask to be put in touch with each lessor-investor to confirm their position to ensure that there is, in fact, an unqualified commitment, and there are no misunderstandings as to the transaction terms.

Leveraged Lease Participants Have Unique Characteristics

A leveraged lease transaction will involve more parties than a non-leveraged one, as stated earlier. At a minimum, in addition to the lessee, the participants will include an equity participant (lessor-investor), a debt participant, and an equipment supplier.

The Equity Participants

An investor in a leveraged lease is referred to as an *equity participant*. Generally, more than one investor is involved on the *equity side* of a leveraged lease. These equity participants, or owners, often act together through a trust arrangement. The equity participants are deemed the beneficial owners of the equipment. The legal title is held by the representative (the trustee) of the trust.

The typical leveraged lease equity participant is an *institutional investor*, such as a bank. Because, however, a leveraged lease can be an attractive investment, many non-financial corporations and, in a limited number of situations, wealthy individuals are also potential lessor-investor candidates.

The Debt Participants

A lender in a leveraged lease transaction is generally referred to as a *debt participant*. It is common for there to be more than one debt participant involved in a particular lease. When this is the case, they frequently form a trust through which they will act. The amount of money each debt participant intends to loan is transferred to the trust, which in turn lends it to the lessor. The loan made to the lessor is generally nonrecourse in nature.

Leveraged lease third-party debt is often supplied by banks or insurance companies.

The debt interest rate is a critical factor in the rent computation, and accordingly, the lease rent quotation is usually premised on an assumed debt interest rate. Thus, the lower the interest rate, the more profit a lessor makes and vice versa, unless you, as the prospective lessee, get the benefit or bear the risk of interest rate variations. In the latter case, typically, the proposal will provide that if the debt interest rate comes in other than assumed, the rent will be adjusted upward or downward to appropriately reflect the variance.

The Underwriter

The lease underwriting business has a relatively low-capital entrance requirement. Because of this, there is an overabundance of *packagers* (underwriters) offering lease underwriting services. These packagers run the gamut from individuals operating out of a home office to investment bankers to specialized lease underwriting firms. Some are well versed in leveraged leasing economics and documentation, and others know little more than the basics. The choice of an underwriter is critical to the success of a transaction, and you should only deal with those with a wealth of experience to ensure leveraged lease financing success.

The Equipment Manufacturer

The equipment manufacturer or distributor involved in a leveraged lease transaction usually does nothing more than sell the agreed-on equipment to the lessor at the negotiated price. Once the full price has been paid, their only obligation is to stand behind its product for any warranty period.

How Different Is the Leveraged Lease Document?

The format of a typical leveraged lease document is essentially the same as that of any other equipment lease. However, the terms and provisions are usually more detailed because the major dollar commitments involved usually dictate that greater attention be paid to each aspect.

Three Advantages to a Lessee in a Leveraged Lease

In certain situations, a leveraged lease transaction offers many benefits for a prospective lessee and may be the best choice in a given situation.

The Rent Can Be More Attractive

In general, a competitively bid leveraged lease transaction will provide a lower cost to a lessee than a comparable term non-leveraged lease. Logically, if a company can borrow at a more favorable interest rate than a lessor, it stands to reason that if the lessor pays part of the equipment's cost with a loan based on the lessee's credit, it can charge lower rents without sacrificing its economic return. There are, of course, exceptions to this rule, and each situation must be examined on its own.

There Is a Better Market for Large Transactions

Major dollar equipment lease financings can generally be arranged more readily by using a leveraged lease structure because the lessor-investor participants only have to come up with a portion of the required equipment cost, the remainder being provided by one or more third-party lenders. And, by forming investor and lender syndicates, they can keep the dollar exposure for each within desired limits.

The Lessors Can Be More Competitive

The type of lessor interested in pursuing a leveraged lease investment is often most concerned over the available equipment ownership tax benefits. As a result, such a lessor may be more willing to be more aggressive on those aspects of a lease transaction not impacting the lease's tax consequences.

Summary

A leveraged lease is typically a complex and sophisticated vehicle for financing capital equipment. The basic concept, however, is not complex—it is simply a lease transaction in which the lessor puts in only a portion, usually 20 to 40 percent, of the funds necessary to buy the equipment and a third-party lender supplies the remainder. Generally, the third-party loan is on a nonrecourse-to-the-lessor basis and ranges from 60 to 80 percent of the equipment's cost. The nonrecourse nature means the lessor has no repayment responsibility even if the lessee defaults, and the loan becomes uncollectible. However, it must be kept in mind that the mechanics of putting a leveraged lease transaction together is generally complex, often involving many parties brought together through intricate document arrangements. The complexity, however, is offset by the transaction structure benefits to both the lessor and lessee.

CHAPTER 7

The Leasing Financial Analysis

Overview

One of the most important considerations for your company as a prospective lessee or borrower in deciding whether to enter into an equipment lease or other financing contract is the financial aspect. Accordingly, you must know how to assess the different financing options from a financial viewpoint to make the right economic decision. And, understanding how a lessor makes their financial determinations will give you better negotiation leverage, all of which is explained in the upcoming sections.

The Importance of Cash Flow and Timing for a Prospective Lessee or Borrower

In making a financial assessment of whether to lease or buy equipment with internal or borrowed funds, you must take the varying cash flows, and their timing, into account for each alternative. Stated simply, how much are the cash inflows and outflows, and when do they occur? The timing of the cash inflows and outflows is critical because of the principle—referred to as the time value of money—that money received earlier is worth more than money received later.

The following example illustrates very simplistically how taking cash flow and its timing into account alters the result of an analysis.

Illustrative example: Cash flow and time value: An equipment user is considering two options: leasing equipment over a seven-year period with an annual rent of 990 U.S. dollars payable at the beginning of each year and buying the equipment using a seven-year loan with 1,000 U.S. dollars annual payments due at each year's end. By choosing to lease, the company would pay out 990 U.S. dollars one year earlier than it would have to pay the required 1,000 U.S. dollar loan payment. If the company could earn, say, 6 percent a year after taxes on its available funds, giving up the 990 U.S. dollars in advance would result in a *loss* of 59.40 U.S. dollars (6% × $990 = $59.40) in the first year. In this case, the advance payment could be said to cost 1,049.40 U.S. dollars ($990 + $59.40 = $1,049.40). Putting other considerations aside, the 1,000 U.S. dollar loan payment would have been less expensive. If the company were able to earn only 1 percent a year after taxes, paying the 990 U.S. dollars would result in only a 9.90 U.S. dollar *loss* (1% × $990 = $9.90). That is, the effective cost of paying the 990 U.S. dollars would have been 999.90 U.S. dollars, instead of 1,049.40 U.S. dollars. In the latter case, the 1,000 U.S. dollar loan payment could be said to be more expensive.

A Lessee Financial Analysis

Once your company has decided it needs certain equipment, you must determine how to finance its acquisition. The following discussion will address the three possible alternatives for an equipment user:

- The user leases the equipment (the leasing alternative)
- The user draws on their general funds to buy the equipment (the purchase alternative)
- The user takes out a specific loan to buy the equipment (the financing alternative)

This section will compare those three financial alternatives by using a common method for taking cash flows and their timing into account, sometimes referred to as the discounted cash flow—or present value—analysis method. The first step will be to compute the periodic costs and tax savings for each alternative. The next step will be to factor in the timing of those cash flows so that there is a basis for comparison by calculating the present value of each alternative's cash flows. To compute the present value of a series of future cash flows, an interest rate—referred to as the discount rate—must be selected to discount the flows back to their present worth. The result will be the present value cost of the alternatives. Because getting to these results involves many computations, the following analysis will center around one hypothetical equipment acquisition situation.

> **Note:** The financial analysis computations from which the examples in this chapter were developed were done on SuperTRUMP, a widely used and top lease analysis computer software program, developed and offered by Ivory Consulting Corporation (www. ivorycc.com). The information from the computer analysis results was at times summarized by the author to aid in the explanation of the concepts described in the text material.

A Typical Equipment User's Financial Alternatives

White Industries wants to acquire a new high-end computer system and can use all available tax benefits. White Industries is considering three financing alternatives—the lease alternative, the purchase alternative, and the financing alternative. Additional facts include (assumed for ease of illustration without regard to whether any applicable tax or other rules will be satisfied are as follows) the following:

General Data

Computer system cost	One million U.S. dollars
Depreciable period	Five years
Residual value	0 U.S. dollars
Investment tax credit	0 percent
Accounting basis:	Accrual
White Industries combined income tax rate (Federal, state, and local)	35 percent
White Industries tax year	Calendar year
Delivery date	January 1, 2019
Depreciation method	MACRS (half-year, DB/SL 200 percent)

Proposed Financial Lease

Lease term	Seven years
Rental payments	200,000 U.S. dollars, payable in seven annual payments in arrears.
Lease simple interest rate	9.1961 percent
Commencement date	January 1, 2019

Proposed Bank Loan

Loan amount	One million U.S. dollars, repayable in seven equal annual payments of 205,405.50 U.S. dollars in arrears
Loan term	Seven years
Long-term interest rate	10.0 percent
Commencement date	January 1, 2019

The Cost of the Leasing Alternative

The first step is to compute the after-tax cost of the various alternatives. Table 7.1 sets out those costs for the leasing alternative.

Table 7.1

Year ending	Rental payments	Tax savings from rent deductions	After-tax cost	Cumulative after-tax cost
December 30, 2019	$ 0	$70,000	$(70,000)	$(70,000)
December 30, 2020	200,000	70,000	130,000	60,000
December 30, 2021	200,000	70,000	130,000	190,000
December 30, 2022	200,000	70,000	130,000	320,000
December 30, 2023	200,000	70,000	130,000	450,000
December 30, 2024	200,000	70,000	130,000	580,000
December 30, 2025	200,000	70,000	130,000	710,000
December 30, 2026	200,000	0	200,000	910,000
Total	$1,400,000	$490,000	$910,000	N/A

Table 7.1 is computed as follows:

- *Rental payments* are the annual payments the lessee must make. These begin in 2020 because the rent is payable annually in arrears.
- *Tax savings from rent deductions* represents the income tax savings White Industries would realize from the rent deductions, computed at White Industries' assumed combined 35 percent income tax bracket (federal, state, and local).
- *After-tax cost* is derived by subtracting the tax savings from the rent deductions from the rental payments.
- *Cumulative after-tax cost* represents the transaction's total after-tax cost as of each year end.

The result is a total after-tax cost of 910,000 U.S. dollars if White Industries leases the computer system.

The Cost of the Purchase Alternative

The next step is to compute the after-tax cost of an outright purchase using internal funds. *Annual depreciation expense* indicated in Table 7.2 is the amount White Industries would be entitled to deduct under MACRS depreciation as the computer owner over a five-year period. The other columns are computed as in the leasing example (Table 7.1):

Table 7.2

Year ending	equity	Annual Depreciation tax expense	Tax savings	After-tax cost	Cumulative After-tax cost
December 30, 2019	$1,000,000	$200,000	$ 70,000	$930,000	$930,000
December 30, 2020	0	320,000	112,000	(112,000)	818,000
December 30, 2021	0	192,000	67,200	(67,200)	750,800
December 30, 2022	0	115,200	40,320	(40,320)	710,480
December 30, 2023	0	115,200	40,320	(40,320)	670,160
December 30, 2024	0	57,600	20,160	(20,160)	650,000
Total	$1,000,000	$1,000,000	$350,000	$650,000	n/a

Comparing Cash Flows

Thus, at this point in the analysis, the purchase alternative seems substantially less expensive than the lease alternatives as its total after-tax cost is only 650,000 U.S. dollars compared with 910,000 U.S. dollars for leasing. However, this ignores the leasing cash flow advantage because, as shown in Table 7.3, the total cost of the lease is less until the seventh year.

Table 7.3 *Cash flow comparison*

Year	Lease cumulative after-tax cost	Purchase cumulative after-tax cost	Lease cash advantage
2019	$(70,000)	$930,000	$1,000,000
2020	60,000	818,000	758,000
2021	190,000	750,000	560,000
2022	320,000	710,000	390,000
2023	450,000	670,000	220,000
2024	580,000	650,000	70,000
2025	710,000	650,000	(60,000)
2026	910,000	650,000	(260,000)

Plainly, leasing does conserve money in the early years, and those available funds could be put to use elsewhere. The resulting earnings on those funds would offset the disparity in total cost between the two alternatives. Thus, it cannot be concluded that leasing is more expensive until the present value of the two alternative's cash flows is compared.

To calculate the present value of the leasing and buying cash flows, White Industries must discount both alternatives' cash flows to their present worth. Choosing a 10 percent annual discount rate and assuming White Industries pays its estimated taxes on April 15, June 15, September 15, and December 15 of each year, the after-tax cash flows for the leasing and purchase alternatives are as follows, as shown in Table 7.4 below:

Table 7.4 *Present value comparison*

Year	Lease		Purchase	
	After-tax cost	Present value	After-tax cost	present value
January 01, 2019	0.00	0.00	1,000,000.00	1,000,000.00
April 15, 2019	(17,500.00)	(17,008.64)	(17,500.00)	(17,008.64)
June 15, 2019	(17,500.00)	(16,729.81)	(17,500.00)	(16,729.81)
September 15, 2019	(17,500.00)	(16,321.77)	(17,500.00)	(16,321.77)
December 15, 2019	(17,500.00)	(15,923.67)	(17,500.00)	(15,923.67)
	70,000.00	65,983.89	930,000.00	934,016.11
January 01, 2020	200,000.00	181,179.00	0.00	0.00
April 15, 2020	(17,500.00)	(15,408.09)	(28,000.00)	(24,852.95)
June 15, 2020	(17,500.00)	(15,166.50)	(28,000.00)	(24,245.80)
September 15, 2020	(17,500.00)	(14,785.85)	(28,000.00)	(23,657.37)
December 15, 2020	(17,500.00)	(14,425.22)	(28,000.00)	(23,080.38)
	130,000.00	121,404.92	112,000.00	95,639.47
January 01, 2021	200,00.00	164,130.23	0.00	0.00
April 15, 2021	(17,500.00)	(13,958.16)	(16,800.00)	(13,399.83)
June 15, 2021	(17,500.00)	(13,729.34)	(16,800.00)	(13,180.16)
September 15, 2021	(17,500.00)	(13,394.47)	(16,800.00)	(12,858.70)
December 15, 2021	(17,500.00)	(13,067.78)	(16,800.00)	(12,545.07)
	130,000.00	109,980.48	67,200.00	51,983.76
January 01, 2022	200,000.00	148,685.24	0.00	0.00
April 15, 2022	(17,500.00)	(12,644.67)	(10,080.00)	(7,283.33)
June 15, 2022	(17,500.00)	(12,437.38)	(10,080.00)	(7,163.93)
September 15, 2022	(17,500.00)	(12,134.03)	(10,080.00)	(8,989.20)

(*Continued*)

Table **7.4** *Present value comparison (Continued)*

December 15, 2022	(17,500.00)	(11,838.08)	(10,080.00)	(8,818.737)
	130,000.00	99,631.08	40,320.00	28,255.19
January 01, 2023	200,000.00	134,693.66	0.00	0.00
April 15, 2023	(17,500.00)	(11,454.78)	(10,080.00)	(6,597.95)
June 15, 2023	(17,500.00)	(11,267.00)	(10,080.00)	(6,459.79)
September 15, 2023	(17,500.00)	(10,992.19)	(10,080.00)	(6,331.50)
December 15, 2023	(17,500.00)	(10,724.09)	(10,080.00)	(6,177.08)
	130,000.00	90,255.60	40,320.00	25,598.32
January 01, 2024	200,000.00	122,018.71	0.00	0.00
April 15, 2024	(17,500.00)	(10,376.86)	(5,040.00)	(2,988.54)
June 15, 2024	(17,500.00)	(10,206.75)	(5,040.00)	(2,939.54)
September 15, 2024	(17,500.00)	(9,957.80)	(5,040.00)	(2,867.85)
December 15, 2024	(17,500.00)	(9,714.93)	(5,040.00)	(2,797.90)
	130,000.00	81,762.37	20,160.00	11,593.83
January 01, 2025	200,000.00	110,536.50	0.00	0.00
April 15, 2025	(17,500.00)	(9,400.38)	0.00	0.00
June 15, 2025	(17,500.00)	(9,246.27)	0.00	0.00
September 15, 2025	(17,500.00)	(9,020.75)	0.00	0.00
December 15, 2025	(17,500.00)	(8,800.74)	0.00	0.00
	130,000.00	74,068.36	0.00	0.00
January 01, 2026	200,000.00	100,134.79	0.00	0.00
	200,000.00	100,134.79	0.00	0.00
Total	910,000	611,253.72	650,000.00	720,947.55

The discounted cash flow analysis clearly reverses the outcome. The leasing alternative's present worth is 611,253.72 U.S. dollars, while the purchase alternative's is 720,947.55 U.S. dollars. Based on this analysis, leasing the computer system would be less expensive than buying with internal funds.

The Financing Alternative

The next step is to calculate the financing alternative's cash flow in the same manner. The computation is the same as the purchase alternative (Table 7.2), with the additional factors being the payment of the 10 percent interest and the tax savings on deducting the interest. The after-tax cost calculations are as follows as shown in Table 7.5 below:

Table 7.5

Year ending	Debt payments	Year-end principal balance outstand ing	10 percent interest on principal	Tax savings (deprecia tion and interest)	Net after- tax cost
December 30, 2019	$ 0.00	$1,000,000.00	$100,000.000	$105,000.00	$(105,000.00)
December 30, 2020	205,405.50	894,594.50	89,459.45	143,310.81	62,094.69
December 30, 2021	205,405.50	778,645.45	77,846.85	94,452.70	110,952.80
December 30, 2022	205,405.50	651,107.80	65,110.78	63,108.77	142,296.73
December 30, 2023	205,405.50	510,813.08	51,081.31	58,198.46	147,207.04
December 30, 2024	205,405.50	356,488.88	35,648.89	32,637.11	172,768.39
December 30, 2025	205,405.50	186,732.27	18,673.23	6,535.63	198,869.87
December 30, 2026	205,405.50	0.00	0.00	0.00	205,405.02
Total	$1,437,838.50	$0.00	$437,838.50	$503,243.47	$934,595.02

The present worth calculation, again using a 10 percent discount rate, results in the following (again assuming estimated all income tax payments are made on April 15, June 15, September 15, and December 15 of each tax year):

Table 7.6 *Present value comparison*

	Lease		Financing	
Year	after-tax cost	present value	after-tax cost	Present value
January 01, 2019	0.00	0.00	0.00	0.00
April 15, 2019	(17,500.00)	(17,008.64)	(26,250.00)	(25,512.96)
June 15, 2019	(17,500.00)	(16,729.81)	(26,250.00)	(25,094.71)
September 15, 2019	(17,500.00)	(16,321.77)	(26,250.00)	(24,482.65)
December 15, 2019	(17,500.00)	(15,923.67)	(26,250.00)	(23,885.51)
	70,000.00	65,983.89	105,000.00	98,975.83
January 01, 2020	200,000.00	181,179.00	205,405.50	186,076.43
April 15, 2020	(17,500.00)	(15,408.09)	(35,827.70)	(31,544.94)
June 15, 2020	(17,500.00)	(15,166.50)	(35,827.70)	(31,027.81)
September 15, 2020	(17,500.00)	(14,785.85)	(35,827.70)	(30,271.04)
December 15, 2020	(17,500.00)	(14,425.22)	(35,827.70)	(29,532.72)
	130,000.00	121,404.92	62,094.69	63,699.91
January 01, 2021	200,00.00	164,130.23	205,405.50	168,566.26
April 15, 2021	(17,500.00)	(13,958.16)	(23,613.17)	(18,834.08)
June 15, 2021	(17,500.00)	(13,729.34)	(23,613.17)	(18,525.33)
September 15, 2021	(17,500.00)	(13,394.47)	(23,613.17)	(18,073.49)

December 15, 2021	(17,500.00)	(13,067.78)	(23,613.17)	(17,632.67)
	130,000.00	109,980.48	110,952.80	95,500.68
January 01, 2022	200,000.00	148,685.24	205,405.50	152,703.83
April 15, 2022	(17,500.00)	(12,644.67)	(15,777.19)	(11,399.85)
June 15, 2022	(17,500.00)	(12,437.38)	(15,777.19)	(11,212.97)
September 15, 2022	(17,500.00)	(12,134.03)	(15,777.19)	(10,939.48)
December 15, 2022	(17,500.00)	(11,838.08)	(15,777.19)	(10,672.66)
	130,000.00	99,631.08	142,296.73	108,478.87
January 01, 2023	200,000.00	134,693.66	205,405.50	138,334.09
April 15, 2023	(17,500.00)	(11,454.78)	(14,549.61)	(9,523.58)
June 15, 2023	(17,500.00)	(11,267.00)	(14,549.61)	(9,367.45)
September 15, 2023	(17,500.00)	(10,992.19)	(14,549.61)	(9,138.98)
December 15, 2023	(17,500.00)	(10,724.09)	(14,549.61)	(8,916.08)
	130,000.00	90,255.60	147,207.04	101,388.00
January 01, 2024	200,000.00	122,018.71	205,405.00	125,316.57
April 15, 2024	(17,500.00)	(10,376.86)	(8,159.28)	(4,838.15)
June 15, 2024	(17,500.00)	(10,206.75)	(8,159.28)	(4,758.84)
September 15, 2024	(17,500.00)	(9,957.80)	(8,159.28)	(4,642.77)
December 15, 2024	(17,500.00)	(9,714.93)	(8,159.28)	(4,529.53)
	130,000.00	81,762.37	172,768.39	106,547.27
January 01, 2025	200,000.00	110,536.50	205,405.50	113,524.03
April 15, 2025	(17,500.00)	(9,400.38)	(1,633.91)	(877.68)
June 15, 2025	(17,500.00)	(9,246.27)	(1,633.91)	(863.29)

(Continued)

Table 7.6 *Present value comparison* (**Continued**)

September 15, 2025	(17,500.00)	(9,020.75)	(1,633.91)	(842.23)
December 15, 2025	(17,500.00)	(8,800.74)	(1,633.91)	(821.69)
	130,000.00	74,068.36	198,869.87	110,119.14
January 01, 2026	200,000.00	100,134.79	205,405.50	102,841.18
	200,000.00	100,134.79	205,405.50	102,841.18
Total	910,000	611,253.72	934,595.02	589,599.23

Comparing Cash Flows

As Table 7.6 shows, the financial alternative results in a present value cost of (598,599.23 U.S. dollars), the least expensive of the three alternatives. This result is not intended to mean that financing with borrowed funds is always the best alternative because the specific result was based on the assumed facts. Rather, it is intended to show how dramatically the present value cash flow analysis alters the result. The financing alternative, with the highest cumulative cost, results in the lowest present worth cost, and the purchase alternative, with the lowest cumulative cost, results in the highest present worth cost.

Understanding the Lessor's Lease Investment Analysis

A lessor, in making their financial analysis, needs to determine what their economic return will be on the leased equipment. The concepts of cash flow and present value also play an important part in the lessor's analysis.

This section will analyze one type of lease, the non-leveraged lease, where the lessor uses their own funds entirely to buy the equipment.

Non-Leveraged Lease

As explained earlier, in a non-leveraged lease, the lessor supplies all the money necessary to buy the equipment from their own funds. Whether this type of investment will make economic sense depends on how profitable the transaction will be to the lessor. Thus, determining the profit—commonly referred to as the rate of return (usually computed on an after-tax basis)—is a threshold issue in any financial lease investment evaluation.

Traditionally, an after-tax lessor's rate of return has been defined as the interest rate—sometimes referred to as the discount rate—that will discount a lease's after-tax cash flows back to a value equal to its initial cash outlay. Or, looking at it another way, it is the rate that, when applied to the original cash investment, will produce the future cash flow amounts generated by the lease.

To explain the investor rate of return analysis approach, we will work through a hypothetical non-leveraged lease example, assuming the following facts:

Equipment Data

Cost	One million U.S. dollars
Depreciable life	Five years
Residual value	0 U.S. dollars
Delivery date	January 1, 2019
Lease commencement date	January 1, 2019
Description	Computer system

Lease Investment Data

Lease term	Seven years
Rental payments	Seven annual payments in arrears, each equal to 200,000 U.S. dollars
ITC	0 percent
Lessor combined income tax rate (federal, state, and local)	35 percent
Depreciation method	MACRS (half-year, DB/SL 200)

Based on those facts, and the assumption that the lessor is an accrual basis taxpayer, Table 7.7 sets out the lessor's cash flow and federal income reports.

Table 7.7

Year ending	Rent income	Annual depreciation	Taxable income	Total taxes_ paid	Equity	Pre-tax cash flow	After-tax cash flow
Dec. 30, 2019	0.00	200,000.00	0.00	0.00	1,000,000.00	(1,000,000.00)	(1,000,000.00)
Dec. 30, 2020	200,000.00	320,000.00	(120,000.00)	(42,000.00)	0.00	200,000.00	242,000.00
Dec. 30, 2021	200,000.00	192,000.00	8,000.00	2,800.00	0.00	200,000.00	197,200.00
Dec. 30, 2022	200,000.00	115,200.00	84,800.00	29,680.00	0.00	200,000.00	170,320.00
Dec. 30, 2023	200,000.00	115,200.00	84,800.00	29,680.00	0.00	200,000.00	170,320.00
Dec. 30, 2024	200,000.00	57,600.00	142,400.00	49,840.00	0.00	200,000.00	150,160.00
Dec. 30, 2025	200,000.00	0.00	200,000.00	70,000.00	0.00	200,000.00	130,000.00
Dec. 30, 2026	200,000.00	0.00	0.00	0.00	0.00	200,000.00	200,000.00
Total	$1,400,000.00	$1,000,000.00	$400,000.00	$140,000.00	$1,000,000.00	$400,000.00	$260,000.00

The columns in Table 7.7 are computed as follows:

- *Annual depreciation* represents the amount of the annual MACRS deduction available to the lessor on the computer as a five-year recovery property and applying the half-year convention (all discussed in Chapter 4).
- *Taxable income* is the result of subtracting the annual depreciation deduction from the rent income. The lessor is an accrual basis taxpayer, so the rent income is accrued for the year ending December 30, 2019, for income tax purposes, resulting in no taxable income for this year ($200,000 rent income – $200,000 depreciation expense = 0), and there would be no tax accrued rent income for the year ending December 30, 2026.
- *Total taxes paid* represents the dollar savings or cost on the income or loss in the *Taxable income* column based on a 35 percent combined income tax rate (federal, state, and local). Where the figure is negative, the lessor reduces their overall tax liability by that amount.
- *After-tax cash flow* results from adjusting *Pre-tax cash flow* by the amount of the taxes paid or saved. Thus, where the *Total taxes paid* figure is negative, this amount is added to *Pre-tax cash flow*; where the *Total taxes paid* figure is positive, this amount is subtracted from *Pre-tax cash flow*.

Once the after-tax cash flows have been calculated, the after-tax rate of return—often referred to as the after-tax yield—can be found by finding the interest rate that will discount the after-tax cash flows back to the cost of the computer, one million U.S. dollars. Here, the lessor will receive an after-tax yield equal to 9.1961 percent.

Summary

The key to a proper lessee lease verses purchase analysis, or a lessors' investment return analysis, is determining the various cash inflows and outflows on a present value basis. Because of the complexity of making these determinations, and the risk of human computation error, it is always advisable to use one of the many computer programs available today for these purposes.

CHAPTER 8

Understanding the New Lease Accounting Rules

Background

During the early years of the equipment leasing business, the accounting profession devoted considerable time and effort discussing how leases should be accounted for, both from the standpoint of the lessor and lessee. There were many inconsistencies and substantive disagreements. Today, the subject of accounting for leases has been addressed by the accounting profession's standard setting body, the Financial Accounting Standards Board (FASB), as set forth in the *Statement of Financial Accounting Standards No. 13-Accounting for Leases*, in effect since 1977. Commonly referred to as FAS No. 13, the rules promulgated established the standards to be followed by lessors and lessees in accounting for and reporting lease transactions.

Since FAS No. 13 was issued, the FASB had been called on to address a wide variety of issues raised by FAS 13 and various amendments and interpretations have been issued to clarify or handle many of the guideline's complex issues. Some of the newly issued amendments and interpretations significantly impact lessees. For example, under the original FASB-promulgated lease accounting rules, some lease transactions, referred to as *operating leases*, or leases that typically were not *full payout* in nature, essentially those in which not all or substantially all of the equipment cost was paid through lease rents, could be treated as *off-balance* sheet transactions by lessees for accounting purposes. That is, if the lease was classified for accounting purposes as an operating, as opposed to a capital (now called a *finance*) lease, discussed in the following sections, it did not have to be reported in the lessee's financial statements as a long-term liability, and the rents could be expensed as they occurred (in effect, off-balance sheet treat-ment), thereby minimizing the impact of the transaction on key finan-cial ratios that may impact the lessee's cost of future funds. One of the significant benefits of off-balance sheet treatment was that a long-term lease, at times, could be used to obtain needed equipment without violating covenants in loan and credit agreements that restricted the amount of long-term indebtedness a lessee may incur. This is essen-tially no longer possible.

One important point for you to be aware of is that the technical aspects of lease accounting are very complex and nuanced for both a lessor and a lessee, and the explanation in this chapter is meant only to provide a general understanding of the accounting rules.

Understanding Lessee Lease Accounting Classifications

Under FAS No. 13, today, a lessee must account for and report a lease in their financial statements as either a *finance* (formerly referred to as a *capital*) lease or an *operating* lease, depending on how the transaction is structured. In certain cases, it may not be advisable for a company to lease equipment because of the accounting treatment impact.

A lease must be treated by a lessee as a finance lease under FAS No.13 if, at its inception, it meets one or more of the following criteria: (i) it provides for a transfer of the property's ownership to the lessee at the end of the lease term, (ii) the lease contains a bargain purchase option, (iii) the lease term is equal to or greater than 75 percent of the property's estimated economic useful life, or (iv) the present value (using, typically, the lessee's incremental borrowing rate) of the *minimum lease payments* at the lease inception is equal to or greater than 90 percent of the excess of the fair value of the leased property (determined at the beginning of the lease). If the lease does not meet any of the aforementioned criteria, it is classified as an operating lease. *Minimum lease payments* include the minimum lease term rental payments stated in the lease and any lessee guarantee of the residual value of the leased equipment at the end of the lease term, whether or not the lessee payment of the guarantee is a pur-chase of the leased equipment.

An operating lease for accounting purposes is like a short-term rental contract, with the lessee reporting the lease payments as operating expenses, but not claiming any depreciation expense. The lessor (the equipment owner), however, can claim the depreciation tax benefits. Finance leases, on the other hand, under the accounting rules are viewed like a financed purchase—in other words, under the lease terms, the lessee may have some of the benefits of ownership, such as charging depreciation expense, and accounting for the asset on the balance sheet as a capital asset.

The Impact on a Lessee of the Lease Accounting Requirements

If a lease is classified as a finance lease, the lessee does not state the rent as an expense item. The lessee must record the lease as an asset and an obligation at an amount equal to the present value (determined as of the beginning of the lease term) of the minimum lease payments during the lease term. *Nonlease components*, payments due under the lease for goods or services separate from the property leased, included in the payments, such as insurance, maintenance, and taxes, that the lessor must pay (passed through costs billed to the lessee) must be included before making the present value computation. If the present value of the minimum lease payments is greater than the property's *fair value* (generally, its purchase cost) determined at the beginning of the lease, then the fair value is to be recorded.

A finance lease must be written off (amortized) by a lessee under certain specific rules, dictated by which of the four finance lease classification criteria is met. If the lease meets the first or second criterion (that is, property ownership is transferred to the lessee at lease end or the lessee has a bargain purchase option), the lessee must write it off in a manner consistent with its usual depreciation practice for assets they own. If the lease does not meet either of these two criteria, the lessee must amortize the property over a period equal to the lease term in a manner consistent with its normal depreciation practice down to a value they expect the property to be worth at the end of the lease. In other words, a lease characterized as a finance (non-operating) lease, for lease accounting purposes, in effect, is to be reported in the lessee's financial statements as though they basically had bought the equipment and taken out a loan to finance its purchase.

For leases categorized as operating leases, prior to the new changes to the original FASB accounting rules, generally, the lease payments could be charged to expense as they become due on a straight-line basis, whether or not they were in fact payable on a straight-line basis. They were treated as off-balance sheet items. Under the recently revised FASB lease accounting rules, which were 10 years in the making, and are now effective for public business entities beginning on January 1, 2019, and for all other entities beginning on January 1, 2020, operating leases, as stated earlier, can no longer qualify as an off-balance sheet item for lessees. That is, as of the applicable updated FAS 13 accounting rule effective dates, most operating lease obligations must be capitalized in the same manner as finance lease obligations and must be included as assets and as liabilities on the balance sheet, which affects some financial measurements, such as earnings before interest, taxes, depreciation, and amortization (commonly referred to as *EBITDA*), as well as operating leverage and interest coverage. Lease payments in the case of leases qualifying as operating leases can, however, be categorized as *non-debt*.

In certain situations, however, if a lease qualifies as a short-term lease, one that has a lease term of 12 months or less and does not have a purchase option the lessee is reasonably certain to exercise, it can be treated in a manner similar to how an operating lease had originally been treated as an off-balance sheet item, that is, not reflected on the lessee's balance sheet. All other leases, in effect, now become a balance sheet item, where the lessee must recognize the rent payments as a long-term liability, which must be amortized over the term of the lease.

It should also be kept in mind that equipment supplied under managed services and fee-per-use agreements, originally thought by some to be treated by customers or obligors as off-balance sheet obligations, may, in fact, depending on the contract provisions, now require treatment similar to that required under traditional lease arrangements.

The Lease Classification Categories for a Lessor

For a lessor, FAS No. 13 now provides that all leases must be categorized as either sales-type leases, direct financing leases, or operating leases. A lease will be classified as a sales-type lease if the lease is classified as a finance lease for the lessee and is to be classified as a direct financing lease only if the lease is classified as a finance lease if, a result of a third-party end-of-lease residual guaranty, the present value of the minimum lease payments test is met. A lease is classified as an operating lease if it is not a direct financing lease or a sales-type lease.

Summary

The *Statement of Financial Accounting Standards No. 13-Accounting for Leases* commonly referred to as FAS No. 13, sets forth the rules to be followed by lessors and lessees in accounting for and reporting lease transactions. FAS No. 13, in effect, says that a lease that transfers substantially all of an asset's ownership benefits and risks to the lessee must be treated by the lessee in the same way as an asset bought with borrowed money is treated (finance lease treatment). On the other hand, the lessor must account for the lease as a sale or a financing. Operating lease obligations were originally not required by lessees to be recorded as balance sheet obligations, but today they must be capitalized in a manner similar to finance lease obligations. That is, they must be included as assets and as liabilities on the balance sheet. Lease payments in the case of leases qualifying as operating leases can, however, be categorized as *non-debt*. The rules are complex, so care must be taken in assessing their impact on an equipment lease transaction.

CHAPTER 9

Negotiating the Lease Document

What Is the Lease's Central Purpose?

Although an equipment lease agreement can involve many complex, highly technical, and sometimes overwhelming concepts, its central purpose is very simple—it is a contract in which an equipment owner, the lessor, transfers the right to use the equipment to another, the lessee, for a period. The lessor retains equipment title.

A lease differs from a conditional sale, an outright sale, or a mortgage type of transaction. Under a conditional sale, the equipment owner finances the sale of the equipment, not merely its use, for the buyer. At the time the agreement is entered into, the equipment seller, in effect, transfers the equipment to the buyer and typically retains the technical legal title until the buyer performs certain conditions, usually the payment of the purchase price in installments. Following satisfaction of the conditions, the equipment owner transfers the title to the buyer.

In an outright sale arrangement, the property owner unconditionally transfers the property, including the title, to the buyer and, at the same time, the buyer pays the seller the full purchase price. In a mortgage situation, a buyer of property borrows from a third-party lender some or all of the money necessary to buy the property. The lender, or mortgagee, as security for the repayment of its loan, requires the borrower, or mortgagor, to give it a security interest in (lien on) the property. The borrower has possession of, and the title to, the property subject to the lender's right to foreclose on the property in the event of a loan default.

The Common Lease Forms

Leases fall into one of two basic formats—the single-transaction lease format and the master lease format. Although both follow the same fundamental structure, the lessor's format choice is dictated by the type of financing transaction, the relationship the lessor anticipates, and its document negotiation strategy. If your company, as a lessee, has developed your own lease forms, the format choice is typically dictated by who has the best negotiating leverage.

> **Recommendation:** If your company, as a lessee, anticipates using leasing as a frequent way to finance your equipment needs, it is advisable to develop your own lease form and make using that form a condition of a financing award. This will save you review time and money and speed up the documentation process. Your lease form should accompany your request-for-bids letter, requiring the bidding lessor to identify any form revisions they will require in or with their proposal.

The Single-Transaction Lease

Lessors, particularly in *vendor* programs (where the lessor has a committed relationship to provide financing for customers of an equipment seller), frequently use a *standard* pre-printed single-transaction lease. The standard lease form has fill-in blanks for those aspects, such as rent, that typically vary with each transaction. Although this type of lease format can be tailored to meet certain required variations, too many changes squeezed into the document margins, or attached as riders, can result in a difficult-to-read document. Traditionally, pre-printed single-transaction leases have been used in small-ticket to mid-sized (typically under 500,000 U.S. dollars in equipment cost) lease financings, but some lessors today use them for much higher dollar transactions.

The pre-printed lease format is particularly attractive for lessors in small dollar lease transactions because it cuts down on drafting and negotiation, and thus helps keep documentation costs, such as legal fees, to a minimum. That can help both parties because the greater the expenses, the less the profit to a lessor, and the greater the overall cost to the lessee. However, using a lessor's pre-printed form lease can be risky for a lessee. They are often one-sided, giving few benefits to the lessee and containing many traps hidden in the fine print, so a lessee must read them carefully.

The Master Lease

A lease format set up to permit future delivered equipment to be easily added is commonly referred to as a master lease. It may be in a pre-printed form or be a document specifically prepared for a particular transaction (a custom lease approach). Traditionally, master lease formats are used in medium-sized (middle market) and large-ticket lease transactions. Once again, savvy lessees prepare their own master lease form, send it with their bid letter, require as a condition of an award that their form be used, and that the lessor proposal identify areas in the master lease form where changes will be requested.

A master lease has two parts: the main, or *boilerplate*, portion contains the provisions that will remain the same from transaction to transaction (such as basic representations, warranties, tax obligations, and maintenance responsibilities), and the second part, sometimes called a *schedule*, contains the items that will vary among transactions (such as equipment type, rent, and options). Typically, the schedule will be short—often only one or two pages—while the main portion may be up to 10 to 40 or more typed pages (if not pre-printed) for a multimillion-dollar transaction. The advantage to using a master lease format is that the parties can document future transactions with a minimum amount of time and expense by merely adding a schedule containing the information pertaining to the specific transaction.

Subjects to Address in Negotiating the Lease

Before starting and during the lease negotiations, you, on behalf of your company as a prospective lessee, must understand the legal, financial, and practical aspects of a lease. Without that understanding, you may inadvertently give up on an issue that is important, be too adamant about a point of little consequence, or miss an issue altogether.

The following discussion identifies issue arears that can arise in a major equipment lease, using the typical provisions found in a net finance lease because it is generally the most comprehensive and complex lease form. Understanding the issues arising in a net finance lease will enable you to deal with virtually any kind of equipment lease.

Identify the Parties to the Lease

The lease should begin by clearly stating each party's full legal name, the jurisdiction in which each is organized, and the mailing address of their principal places of business. This will prevent disputes as to who is intended to be bound by the contract.

The Factual Summary

When the lease document is typed specifically for a particular trans-action, and is not a pre-printed form, it is always a good idea for it, at the document beginning, to summarize the basic facts surround-ing the transaction. The summary provides a valuable future reference for individuals not involved at the time the lease was negotiated. For example, the summary might describe the equipment purchase con-tract your company entered into with the equipment vendor prior to the lease transaction and state that the right, but not the obligation, to buy the equipment has been assigned to the lessor as part of the transaction.

Definitions of the Key Terms

The lease should define in one section the fundamental terms used repeat-edly in the lease agreement that have special meaning, preferably at the doc-ument's beginning. For example, terms such as *fair market purchase value, fair market rental value, stipulated loss value,* and *termination value* will usually have certain meanings in a particular transaction, and the parties must agree on their meaning to prevent future ambiguities. Using such a definition section permits the parties to locate definitions more readily and lessens the risk that an important term will accidentally be left undefined.

Dealing with Future-Delivered Equipment

If you want to enter into a lease well before the equipment's delivery date, your document must provide for a way of putting the equipment on lease when it arrives.

Putting Future-Delivered Equipment Under the Lease

When there is a long lead-time for equipment delivery and you want to ensure that your lease financing is in place when it arrives, you must get the lease signed and have included a method for easily putting the equipment under lease. The simplest way is to draft a lease provision in which you will notify the lessor in writing of the equipment's delivery and its acceptability for lease, which, when received by the lessor, will automatically put the equipment under lease and, thereby, authorize the lessor to pay your company's equipment vendor. The notification is usually in what is referred to as an *acceptance certificate*, a written statement that lists the equipment delivered and states that your company has accepted it for lease as of a specified date.

> **Recommendation:** To cover any problems with the equipment acceptability to you when it arrives, and ensure that you will not be required to put it under lease unless its condition is satisfactory, your future-delivered equipment provision should make it clear that your company has the option to reject the equipment if it is not in acceptable condition or otherwise does not conform to your vendor purchase arrangement.

Non-Utilization and Commitment Fees

It is not unusual, when you have the right to reject equipment to be delivered in the future, for the lessor to ask for a non-utilization fee or a commitment fee, as compensation for holding available funds for your company to offset its loss of the investment opportunity.

A non-utilization fee compensates a lessor for funds committed to future-delivered equipment that remain unused at the end of the commitment period. Usually, the fee is expressed as a percentage of originally estimated equipment cost and is payable in a lump sum at the end of the commitment period. If all or an agreed-on portion of the funds are used, the lessee owes nothing.

A non-utilization fee arrangement has risks for you as a lessee. An unexpectedly high equipment purchase cost (whether from a mistaken estimate or a price escalation) or a delivery delay may give the lessor the right to exclude equipment from the lease. If this happens, you could end up paying a non-utilization fee based on the unused funds remaining at the end of the commitment period. It is not, however, generally considered unreasonable for the lessee to bear this type of risk.

> **Recommendation:** If you are faced with a non-utilization fee arrangement, you can lessen the payment impact from equipment exclusions by negotiating a commitment percentage leeway such that the fee would be payable only to the extent that greater than, say, 10 percent of the committed funds are not used.

The other approach, a commitment fee, is more commonly used. Under this arrangement, you pay a flat fee at the time the lease is entered based on the total equipment cost involved for the lease funding commitment. Generally, the fee is expressed as a percentage of total cost, commonly ranging from 0.375 to 1 percent. Because the commitment fee pays a lessor for holding funds available, you can freely elect not to put equipment on lease.

> **Recommendation:** The best time to negotiate a reduction or elimination of any non-utilization or commitment fee is during the lease proposal stage, making it, for example, a condition of a lease financing award. As already stated, this is the time when you have the most negotiating leverage.

Minimum Grouping Requirements

When a lease involves many less expensive equipment items to be delivered over a long period, a lessor may require a minimum equipment acceptance grouping to reduce its administrative handling expenses. For example, you may not be able to accept equipment for lease in aggregate cost groups of, say, less than 100,000 U.S. dollars.

An equipment grouping requirement can cause serious problems for you. For example, if the dollar minimum was set high, you may have to manipulate deliveries to avoid having to pay for equipment for which your company does not yet have lease funding until the specified amount is accumulated.

> **Recommendation:** If you are confronted with a minimum dollar amount equipment grouping requirement, ask for a *best efforts* qualification, which, after using your best efforts to assemble the required minimum, becomes impractical to do so; you will be permitted to have a smaller amount accepted.

The Lease Term

Clearly, the period of permitted use, the term of lease, is a critical aspect of your lease financing. Generally, there are two basic periods: (1) a main lease term, referred to as the *base lease term*, the *primary lease term*, or the *initial lease term* and (2) a renewal term. Some transactions also call for an *interim lease term*, beginning when the equipment becomes subject to lease until the start of a predetermined base term. The interim term concept is frequently used when many equipment items will go on lease at various times. For example, the base term may start on January 1, 20XX, for all equipment delivered during the prior three-month period. By consolidating the start of the primary lease term to one date after which all equipment will be delivered, administrative work and rent payment mechanics are simplified.

> **Recommendation:** It is usually best to eliminate any interim lease term, unless other factors like a quantity of varying equipment deliveries dictate otherwise. Although it extends your period of use, it also increases your cost of lease financing.

The Rent Payment Structure

Because when the rent payments are due and how much you must pay are key elements of every lease transaction, your lease must precisely set out in detail those terms. For example, a 10-year lease may call for rent to be payable in 20 consecutive, level, semi-annual in arrears payments, each payment to be equal to 2 percent of the total cost of the equipment.

Payment Mechanism

To avoid problems, the lease should specify: (1) where the rent is payable, such as at the lessor's place of business; (2) the form of payment, such as in immediately available U.S. funds; and (3) when it is to be deemed received by the lessor, such as when deposited in a U.S. mailbox or when the lessor has received immediately available funds. Unless the lease specifies those terms, you run the risk of the lessor claiming a technical default based on what the lessor deems to be an incorrect or late payment.

Fixing the Rental Amount and Costs

Other than using fixed dollar amounts, lease rent may be expressed as a percentage of equipment cost. In this way, for equipment to be delivered after the lease is signed, the rent does not have to be recalculated if the purchase price varies from that anticipated. For example, if the annual rent is expressed as 2 percent of equipment cost, changes in cost will not require a lease amendment.

Additionally, your lease should state what expenses may be included, or *capitalized*, as part of the financed equipment *cost*. A prospective lessor with ample funds available will often be eager to include more expenses (*soft* costs) into the rent computation cost base, such as including sales taxes, freight charges, and installation costs. If, however, their money supply is limited, they will probably want to exclude the extras if the *soft* costs could be substantial, or they may not be willing to exceed a certain dollar amount because doing so would dilute their equipment collateral value protection.

Recommendation: Because a prospective lessor willingness to finance soft cost can vary with each transaction, you should define the ground rules in the proposal letter stage to eliminate potential misunderstandings or misconceptions.

Tax Law Rental Adjustment

When a lessor's economic return depends in part on anticipated equipment ownership tax benefits, they may want to be able to make rent adjustments if unexpected tax law changes occur that adversely affect their return. For example, the lease might incorporate a provision that would allow the lessor to adjust the rent to maintain their *yield and after-tax cash flow*. Instead of a yield and after-tax cash flow criteria, leases sometimes use a maintenance of earnings or net return standard. In addition to adjusting the rent, a prospective lessor will also want to adjust values that are based on the rent, such as termination or stipulated loss values.

Recommendations:

- You should always have your lease clearly state the exact formula to be used in making any rent adjustment to enable an independent verification of any of the lessor's computations by, for example, an independent accounting firm. Terms providing for rent adjustments to maintain a lessor's *yield* or *earnings,* for example, do not have standard meanings and can be subject to many interpretations.
- If your lessor has the right to adjust the rent up in the event of an adverse change in the tax laws to compensate for any loss, you should request the right to have the rent adjusted downward if there is a tax law change that is economically favorable to the lessor.

Payment Conditions

Typically, your lease will state that the rent payment obligation is absolute and unconditional, requiring, in effect, that your company pay the rent in full and on time, regardless of any claim it may have against the lessor. Commonly referred to as a *hell or high-water* obligation, the provision at first reading shocks many new prospective lessees. The provision, however, is not as troublesome as it seems initially because it does not prevent a lessee from independently bringing a lawsuit against the lessor on any claim.

> **Recommendation:** Although not technically necessary, some prospective lessees insert a statement in a hell or high-water provision to the effect that any rights of action it may have for damages caused by the lessor will exist, regardless of the hell or high-water rent commitment.

The Lessor's Right to Receive Reports

A lessor, to be able to monitor the transaction, may want the right to receive certain reports from your company, such as financial reports, accident reports, lease conformity reports, equipment location reports, and third-party claim reports. These will enable the lessor to stay on top of the transaction.

> **Recommendation:** You should ensure that the time between the date when the information is gathered and when it is due is adequate for its preparation and submission to avoid a potential default situation.

Financial Reports

One of the ways a lessor will monitor your company's financial condition during the lease term is to require your company to periodically submit financial reports, such as current balance sheets and profit and loss statements, if they are not publicly available. If your company does not have audited financial statements prepared, typically, a lessor will accept tax returns.

Accident Reports

A lessor will typically require your company to immediately notify them of every significant or potentially significant accident involving the leased equipment, whether the damage is to the equipment or to persons or other property because it is not uncommon for a lessor to be sued solely on the basis of their ownership interest.

> **Recommendation:** You should limit your company's accident notification responsibility only to incidents involving serious accidents. One approach is to set an estimated damage dollar amount below which notification is not required.

Equipment Location Reports

Lessors typically require a lessee to prepare and submit equipment location reports so that they can periodically inspect the leased equipment, particularly when the lessee has an obligation to maintain it. If the location is known, it is easy for the lessor to *drop in* to check up on its condition.

> **Recommendation:** Require a lessor to provide your company with a written notice before it makes any inspection, that it will comply with any premises work or other rules that may be applicable, and that any access be limited to normal business hours.

Third-Party Claim Reports

Generally, a lessor will require that your company notifies them of any tax liens or other third-party claims imposed on the equipment, viable or not, so that they have the opportunity to protect their secured position and equipment.

Other Reports

A lessor will typically have the right to request reports that may be determined to be necessary in the future because unforeseeable events may require that the lessor receive certain additional information concerning the equipment.

> **Recommendation:** You should have any general report obligation be qualified to that of only reasonable information relevant to the lease transaction.

Equipment Maintenance and Alterations

Equipment Maintenance

A lease will specify which party has the obligation for equipment maintenance and what will be acceptable maintenance. Many types of leases, such as net finance leases, will put the normal maintenance responsibilities on the lessee. In addition, usually, the lease will often describe lessee maintenance requirements in terms of the condition in which the equipment must be maintained, such as to keep the equipment in *good working order, ordinary wear and tear excepted*. Unfortunately, this type of general requirement can be difficult to comply with because it is somewhat vague, and more specific guidelines should be negotiated.

Recommendations:

- If you will use the equipment in a manner that may cause extra wear and tear, the maintenance provision should exclude ordinary wear and tear resulting from your company's intended use.
- If the equipment's manufacturer provides maintenance instructions, that may be a good lease benchmark for you to agree to.
- In specialized maintenance situations, it is advisable for you to get expert advice to avoid mistakes and potential default situations.
- If the lease permits the lessor access to your company's maintenance records, you should limit access to normal business hours and then only after an advance written notice is provided and also require that the lessor comply with any premises work or other rules that may be applicable.

Equipment Alterations

A lessor typically inserts the right to prohibit a lessee from making equipment alterations not related to normal maintenance because an alteration could affect the equipment's market value and impair its value to the lessor following the end of the lease term.

Recommendation: You should ensure that your company can make any alteration that may be needed by obtaining the lessor's consent, which consent cannot be unreasonably withheld, and that, unless otherwise agreed to, any alteration removable without causing material damage will remain your company's property.

A Lessee Should Require Certain Key Assurances

While the lessor will require certain key assurances from your company as a lessee in the form of representations and warranties, you should also consider requiring the lessor to make similar representations and warranties, something often overlooked by prospective lessees.

That the Lessor Has the Transactional Authority to Lease the Equipment

Even though a leasing company presents itself to the public as being in the leasing business, there may be restrictions, such as in a credit agreement, prohibiting the lessor from entering into particular types of transactions. Also, a prospective lessor may have to go through prescribed internal procedures before a lease is, in fact, an authorized transaction. Violating any restrictions or procedures could jeopardize your right to continue using the equipment. Although an appropriate representation from a lessor will not guarantee there will be no use interference, it will provide your company with a ground on which to base a claim in the event of a problem.

In underwritten transactions, it is possible that some of the lessor-investors, *equity participants*, will not be in the leasing business *per se*. Many corporations, for example, invest in leases on an irregular basis as equity participants, and if the lessor corporation has not obtained all the appropriate internal approvals for the transaction, a lessee may have some enforceability or other lease problems. Thus, it is particularly important in underwritten transactions for you to secure a representation that the transaction has been duly authorized by any lessor-investor.

That the Equipment Will Be Paid For

The lease should include a statement by the lessor, particularly when the lease is executed in advance of equipment delivery, that it will pay for and lease the equipment to your company. While a firm commitment will not guarantee that funds will be available, it will assist in a legal action for damages in the event the lessor does not follow through.

> **Recommendation:** A lessor payment commitment representation is particularly important when you are dealing with smaller, less well-financed leasing companies. It cannot, however, be relied on exclusively if the dollar amount of the equipment involved is significant, or last-minute funding problems could cause a budgeting disruption for your company. Thus, the reputation and financial background of a prospective lessor should be investigated before you make the lease award to ensure that funding risk is at a minimum.

That There Will Be No Interference with the Equipment's Use

Your right to the quiet enjoyment and peaceful possession (full unrestricted use) of the equipment during the lease period is fundamental, provided, of course, you are not in default under the lease and you should require a representation to that effect.

> **Recommendation:** The lessor should provide you with a representation that the equipment will be, and will remain, free of all liens and encumbrances, except those of which you are aware, such as the debt in a leveraged lease, to help ensure there will not be any interference with your company's equipment use from any lessor third-party creditors.

It Is Advisable for a Lessee to Get an Assignment of Product Warranties

Where equipment is supplied by a manufacturer, subcontractor, or supplier, you may, under the lease provisions, be responsible for defects occurring during or existing at the end of the lease term, even though they were caused by the manufacturer, subcontractor, or supplier.

Recommendations:

- To prevent any exposure from any defect responsibility, and because manufacturer warranties run to the equipment purchaser (in the case of a lease, the lessor), you should obtain an assignment of any warranty rights that the lessor would have as equipment owner against any manufacturer, subcontractor, or supplier during the lease term. If these rights are not assignable because, for example, of a warranty restriction, you should have the power to obligate the lessor to sue on your behalf to enforce any warranty rights if deemed necessary.
- If you find it necessary to have the right to require the lessor to sue in their name because, for example, the product warranty rights cannot be assigned, that right should be coupled with the right to control the action, including the selection of counsel and the grounds of the lawsuit.

The Party with the Risk of Loss Should Be Specified

Generally, your company, as a lessee, will bear the risk of equipment loss, whether due to damage, theft, requisition, or confiscation, because you have the equipment. Net finance leases, for example, frequently require the lessee to guarantee that the lessor will receive a minimum amount of money, usually referred to as the *stipulated loss value* or *casualty value*, if there is an equipment loss. The stipulated loss value, which decreases as the lease term runs, is calculated so that the lessor will not have to report a loss on its books. That obligation basically puts your company, as a lessee, in the position of being the equipment's ultimate insurer.

Recommendations:

- Where the lease imposes a stipulated loss obligation, you should (1) request an offset against amounts due for any insurance proceeds or other awards resulting from the loss and (2) make sure your obligations, including rent, under the lease as to the affected equipment, terminate as of the loss date.

- When a stipulated loss provision is incorporated, you should insist on a clear definition of the term *loss*, because it can be susceptible of various interpretations. Generally, unless a defined *loss* has occurred, the rent must continue with the possible result that you will be paying on unusable equipment. Typically, *loss* means destruction to the extent the equipment is no longer usable to a lessee. It is also worth noting that loss for the use intended may be somewhat less than actual total destruction. Thus, you should be careful in agreeing to the ground rules.

- If your company must repair equipment damaged by a third party at your own expense, you should insist on the right to claim any money received, at least up to the cost incurred, from the party causing the damage.

Responsibility for Certain General Taxes

In a typical net finance lease, the lessee will be responsible for paying taxes imposed by any local, state, or federal taxing authority, other than taxes on the net income of the lessor. Some taxes can be substantial, so you should identify what they are and should take into account any tax payment obligations when determining your effective leasing cost.

Recommendations:

- Frequently, lease agreements will require a lessee to pay equipment related taxes that, by law, the lessor must pay. If a lessor is improperly assessed by a taxing authority and refuses to institute a proceeding to correct the problem, your company may still have to pay an incorrect assessment. Thus, you should require a right to be able to have any tax assessment contested or reviewed.

- Your lease should require that the lessor timely notifies your company in writing of potential or actual imposition of any taxes or similar assessments on the equipment, so they can participate at the earliest possible time in any tax contest.

Protecting the Lessor's Tax Benefits

Generally, the parties to a lease will want the transaction to be classified as a *true* lease for federal income tax purposes (see Chapter 5). It is absolutely essential, therefore, that the lease be in a form that ensures the desired tax treatment will not be endangered.

If a *lease* does not qualify as a true tax lease, the lessor will undoubtedly lose the ownership tax benefits, such as depreciation. Because such a loss can turn a favorable transaction into a highly unfavorable one, sophisticated tax lessors try to build protections into the lease documentation in two basic ways—prohibiting inconsistent actions and filings and requiring tax indemnifications.

Inconsistent Actions and Filings Are Prohibited

Typically, a tax-oriented lease will prohibit a lessee from taking any action or filing any documents, including income tax returns, that would be inconsistent with the true lease intent. Normally, this does not present a problem for lessees because, by doing so, they could lose their right to deduct the rent charges as an expense—often the reason the transaction was structured as a lease.

Tax Indemnifications: Designed to Protect the Lessor's Economics

The second way lessors protect themselves against tax benefit losses is through tax indemnification provisions. Typically, these provisions require the lessee to pay the lessor an amount of money that, after taxes, will put them in the same economic position as before the loss.

Tax indemnification provisions can be extremely complex and, to properly assess their effect and workability, you must understand how ownership tax benefits can be lost. Basically, there are three ways: through acts or omissions of the lessor, through acts of omissions of the lessee, or through a change in tax law. For obvious reasons, lessors would like to put the economic burden of a loss or inability to claim all of the expected tax benefits on the lessees, regardless of the cause. Savvy lessees, however, object to assuming the entire burden, and, as a result, a compromise is usually reached.

It is fairly standard in true leases to include a tax indemnity based on the lessee's acts or omissions. An indemnity based on the lessor's acts or omissions is rare, and you should not agree to such an indemnity. The third situation giving rise to potential tax problems, a change (either retroactively or prospectively) in law, can go either way, usually depending on the overall bargaining position of the parties.

Tax Law Changes

How significant is assuming the risk of equipment ownership tax benefit losses resulting from changes in tax law? To begin with, it should be recognized that the *risk* breaks down into a retroactive risk and a prospective risk. That is, changes that affect equipment already delivered and those that affect equipment to be delivered in the future. Although rare, there has been, in the last few years, a retroactive tax law change.

> **Observation:** Prospective lessees have, at times, successfully shifted the burden of an unfavorable-to-lessor retroactive change in tax laws to a prospective lessor by arguing that it is a *normal* leasing business risk that a lessor should assume. There is some logic to this position.

What about prospective changes in tax law affecting equipment that a lessor has assumed available in making their commitment to lease, but that has not yet been delivered? In this case, the risk does not really have to be assumed by either party. For example, the lessor could be given the right to adjust the rent upward an appropriate amount if there is adverse change in the tax benefits before the equipment arrives or have the right to exclude affected equipment. The lessee, in turn, could exclude the equipment if the adjusted rent is too high or, if the lessor has the right to exclude equipment, to have the right to have it included at an adjuster lease rate. Alert prospective lessees usually make sure when a rent adjustment right is given that the lessor will have to make a downward adjustment if there is an increase in the available tax benefits.

> **Recommendation:** If a lessor excludes equipment based on a tax law change, you should ensure that any non-utilization fee excludes the cost of equipment not leased as a result of a lessor's change-in-law exclusion right.

Tax Loss Payment Formula

When a lease includes a tax indemnification provision for the lessor's loss of any anticipated equipment ownership tax benefits, the provision often contains a method for determining the amount a lessee must pay. The provisions are typically broad in scope and provide for a payment that, after deduction of all fees, taxes, and other charges payable as a result of the indemnification payment, will put the lessor in the same economic position as before the loss. Frequently, this will be expressed as paying the lessor enough money to maintain the lessor's *net return*. Unfortunately, terms of this nature, as already suggested, can have many meanings to different people. For example, using a standard such as *total earnings*, *discounted rate of return*, or *after-tax cash flow* can be interpreted in different ways. So, if your company's lease has a tax loss adjustment provision, it should define the adjustment criteria and provide a precise formula for determining the amount of the loss and any required adjustments.

> **Recommendation:** If you must agree to a tax indemnification provision, make sure that any lessor-made adjustment can be verified, at your option, by, say, an independent accounting firm.

The Tax Loss Indemnity Date

The lease will typically identify the time when a lessee becomes obligated to pay any tax indemnity, which could be when the lessor discovers the problem or when the tax benefit loss has been established by the final judgment of a court or administrative agency having jurisdiction over the matter.

Recommendations:

- You should avoid any tax indemnity provision that obligates your company to make any tax indemnification payment until the lessor has actually incurred, or is about to incur, an out-of-pocket-expense.
- You should have a right to require the lessor to contest any tax claim that will trigger an indemnification payment; otherwise, a lessor could decide not to defend against a claim because they will not ultimately have to pay it.
- If you have the right to force a lessor to contest a tax claim, you should also have the right to the return of any amount that your company had to pay before a final resolution, if the lessor later, without justification or consent, settles or discontinues the action.

Equipment Return

The lease will often specify where the equipment is to be returned, the return condition, and who will bear the delivery expense. If, at the lease's end, a lessor, for example, unexpectedly had to pay for the transportation of 200 trucks from 10 of a lessee's plants scattered up and down the East Coast to a central sale point in the Midwest, their profit margin could be noticeably affected. Although who pays for shipping expenses varies with each transaction, it is not unusual for a lessee to pay only for shipping charges to a general transportation shipping point near where the equipment is used.

When the leased equipment is returned, a dispute can arise over whether the equipment's condition meets the standards required in the lease. If a lessor determines that a lessee did not properly maintain the equipment, they can insist that the lessee pay for any repairs necessary to restore the equipment. The best approach for a lessee is to set an objective, easy-to-measure *outside* standard: for example, agreeing that an aircraft under lease will be returned with no less than 50 percent of remaining engine operation time before the next major overhaul. Where an easily measurable objective criterion is not available, the parties might agree to use an independent equipment appraiser to assess the equipment's condition. The lease can either identify the equipment appraiser or set out a method to select appraisers if their services become necessary. A selection method can call for each party to pick an appraiser at the appropriate time, and, if the two selected appraisers cannot reach an agreement, the parties will then jointly select a third independent appraiser whose opinion will be final and binding.

Recommendations:

- You should be cautious about giving a lessor the right to store equipment on your company premises at the end of a lease until a buyer or new lessee can be found. If you must agree to do so, put a time limit on how long it may be so stored, and make sure you have no responsibility for insurance or loss while in storage. And, you may want to consider charging the lessor a storage rent.
- You must carefully consider the potential expense exposure in agreeing to return equipment to a particular return point, particularly when many items are involved. Having the right to choose between alternative return locations may also be advisable. Circumstances can change, and it may turn out to be more practical to transport the equipment to, for example, the nearest railhead instead or the nearest truck pickup point.

Events of Default

If a problem arises that would jeopardize a lessor's rights or interest in the lease or the equipment, the lessor will want to be able to end the lease, and take other action as may be appropriate, such as reclaiming the equipment. The various *problem* situations that could give rise to this type of lessor right are invariably clearly specified in every lease agreement and are referred to as *events of default*.

Where There Is a Nonpayment of Rent

A lessee's failure to pay the rent, when and in the amount due, is always an event of default.

> **Recommendation:** Your company, as a lessee, should require both a reasonable overdue rent payment grace period and a lessor written notice requirement, along with a cure period, before any event of default can be acted on. For example, in the case of a rent payment default, the lease could provide that the failure to pay the rent will not result in an event of default until a period, say 30 days, after your company has received a written notice from the lessor of the nonpayment and the default has not been cured.

When There Is an Unauthorized Transfer

The lease will often provide that if the lessee assigns or transfers the lease agreement or the equipment without the lessor's consent, that will be an event of default. Lessors enter into leases relying on the quality and reputation of the lessee so that if assignments or transfers could result in the equipment ending up in the hands of an unacceptable third party, for example, someone will use the equipment in a high wear operation, that could seriously jeopardize the equipment's anticipated residual value.

> **Recommendation:** Your company's lease should allow you to assign or transfer the lease and the equipment with the lessor's prior written consent, which should not be unreasonably withheld, and certainly in the case your company is acquired.

When There Is a Failure to Perform an Obligation

A lease will invariably provide for a lease event of default if the lessee fails to observe or perform any general condition or agreement in the lease.

Recommendation: You should minimize any general obligation default risk by requiring that the breach be *material* before it gives rise to a default event and require, as with a rent payment default, that the lessor give you at least 30 days' prior written notice cure period before any default can be declared.

When the Lessee Has Made a Misrepresentation

A lessor will often require the lessee to represent certain facts that a lessor deems critical to their decision to enter into the lease. Any misrepresentation of a material nature could subject a lessor to a risk that would not otherwise have assumed had they known the actual facts, and is often listed as an event of default, something to which a lessee may have to agree.

When the Lessee Is Going Bankrupt

A court order or decree declaring the lessee bankrupt or insolvent; the appointment of a receiver, liquidator, or trustee in bankruptcy for a lessee under any state or federal law; any similar action that would expose the leased equipment to a third-party claim or otherwise endanger the lessor's position or any voluntary act by the lessee that would lead to any of these events is typically listed as an event of default. The bankruptcy rules, however, control the lessor's ability to act to reclaim its equipment in a bankruptcy situation.

Lessor Remedies Following an Event of Default

The lease will typically set out what remedies a lessor can pursue if a lessee defaults under a lease. Although doing so will not necessarily guarantee a lessor that a particular action will be permitted if the parties end up in court, it will put a lessee on notice, and thus may weigh against any lessee objection.

Lease agreements incorporate many types of default remedies, usually representing nothing more than a commonsense approach to dealing with the default issue. The various remedies listed in a lease sometimes overlap. Typically, the remedies are listed as court action, termination of the lease, storage, redelivery, sale, and right to hold or re-lease the equipment and liquidated damages. And, generally, other than the liquidated damage computation, these should be of little concern to a lessee because they have defaulted in their lease obligations.

Although there are no industry standard formulas used to measure the damages that a lessor would suffer because of a lessee's default, all formulas typically attempt to achieve the same result—the payment of an amount equal to the present value of the aggregate remaining rentals that the lessor would have received, but for the default, reduced by the equipment's fair market sales value. A prescribed per annum discount rate, such as the prime commercial lending rate in effect at the time of termination, is incorporated into the liquidated damage *formula* for present worth computation purposes.

A Lessor's Lease Assignment Rights

Prospective lessors frequently ask for the right to assign their interest in a lease and the equipment at any time during the term, to, for example, a lender or lease purchaser. While a general assignment right sometimes makes prospective lessees uneasy, this should not cause concern if it is properly negotiated. To help protect your company's lease rights, you should require that any assignment not adversely affect your company's lease rights, and the original lessor's lease obligations.

> **Recommendation:** You may want to consider some control over a lessor lease assignment, such as prohibiting assignment, without your company's prior written consent, to any of your company's banks or lending institutions to avoid the possibility of restricting your company's borrowing capability.

Some Lessee Rights You Will Want Built into Your Lease

Consider having options, typically agreed to by lessors, built into your lease that allow you to have control over the use of the leased equipment, such as equipment purchase, sublease, upgrade, lease renewal, and lease termination rights.

Right to Sublease

If you have the right to sublease equipment, you will be in the best position to lessen or eliminate the impact of paying rent on assets that become unproductive because of changes in use needs during the lease term. If there are no sublease restrictions, such as limited to transfers to affiliated companies only, you will have the maximum cost flexibility to manage equipment no longer needed.

> **Recommendation:** If you have a right to sublease your leased equipment to a third party, avoid agreeing to any exercise conditions, such as having to obtain the lessor's prior written sublease consent. Time wasted waiting for a consent could result in lost revenue. But, if you must obtain the lessor's consent, provide that it cannot be unreasonably withheld.

The Right to Buy Your Leased Equipment at Fair Market Value

An option that gives a lessee the right to buy the equipment for its fair market value at lease end is typically found in lease agreements. Although the term *fair market value* appears self-explanatory, it is always advisable for there to be a workable method for its determination. Generally, the *fair market value* of an item of equipment is the amount that a willing buyer under no compulsion to purchase would pay a willing seller under no compulsion to sell in the open market. As a practical matter, however, how is the value actually determined between a lessor and a lessee? Failing agreement between the parties, typically, it is done through an equipment appraisal. And, often a lease will provide a name of an independent appraiser who will evaluate the equipment at the appropriate time. Alternatively, the parties to the lease can provide that each party can select an independent appraiser to come in and make an assessment when necessary. If the two appraisers cannot agree on a satisfactory value, then typically they must jointly select a third appraiser, whose opinion will be binding.

> **Recommendation:** A fair market value purchase option can be an expensive way for your company to acquire equipment that

typically has a strong resale value. If a strong end-of-lease equipment value is anticipated, consider asking for a purchase price *cap* to limit how much you would have to pay. For example, have the right to buy the equipment at fair market value or 30 percent of the equipment's original cost, whichever is less. However, too low a cap can present a true lease treatment tax problem (see Chapter 5).

The Right to Buy the Equipment at a Fixed Price

When equipment has traditionally maintained a favorable re-sale value, many companies refuse to lease because a fair market purchase option coupled with the lease rents could result in an economically unfavorable way of acquiring it. To address this issue, a fixed-price purchase option is sometimes given to induce them to lease. Under a fixed-price purchase option, commonly referred to as a *call*, a lessee can buy the equipment at the end of the lease for a predetermined price. The price is usually expressed as a percentage of the equipment's original cost. For example, the lessee may have the right to buy designated equipment for 35 percent of the cost. In this way, a lessee knows the maximum amount of money they will have to spend if they want to buy the equipment when the lease is over.

A lessee fixed-price purchase option can cause a lease to fail to be characterized as a true lease for federal income tax purposes. If the exercise price is so low, the lessee may, in effect, have a bargain purchase right, and the Internal Revenue Service (IRS) may be able to challenge successfully its status as a true tax lease (see Chapter 5).

The Right to Renew the Lease at Fair Rental Value

Providing a lessee with the right to renew a lease at the equipment's fair market rental value at the time of renewal is acceptable, both from the standpoint of the IRS and, generally, a lessor. The determination of fair market rental value can be made in a manner similar to that of the determination of the fair market purchase value, through independent appraisal at the time of the intended renewal.

Recommendation: If the leased equipment is vital to your company's operations, make sure the lease renewal terms are adequate to cover any anticipated needs. For example, if a four-year renewal is desirable, an option that would allow a selection of two two-year periods, four one-year periods, one one-year period followed by a three-year period, or a four-year period would provide a great deal of flexibility as to term and as to rental rate. A structure such as this would give your company the ability to limit its renewal costs in a high rental market or to *lock in* for a longer period in a low rental market.

The Right to Renew the Lease at a Fixed Price

Prospective lessees sometimes request a fixed-price renewal option for the same reason that a fixed-price purchase option may be requested. By knowing in advance the exact dollar amount of the renewal rents, they know where they would stand if they wanted to continue to use the equipment beyond the main lease term. This would, of course, not be possible with fair market renewal option. A fixed-price renewal right, however, may result in adverse tax consequences (see Chapter 5). Thus, the amount of fixed renewal option must be carefully considered.

The Right to Terminate the Lease

It is not uncommon for a prospective lessee to want the ability to terminate a lease early, particularly when they believe the equipment could become technically obsolete or surplus to their needs before the lease would normally end. When this right is granted, the lessee frequently will be required to pay the lessor a predetermined amount of money, commonly referred to as the *termination value*, upon exercise. Because most lessors do not like to grant termination rights, the termination amount is usually high.

Recommendation: If you are going to request an early termination option, the time to ask for it and agree on its terms and values is in the proposal stage, when and the termination values should be submitted with a lessor's proposal so that they can be compared with those of other lessor proposals.

The Right of First Refusal

A purchase *right of first refusal* is sometimes used as an alternative to a fair market value purchase option, although not as desirable. Under this option, a lessee is given the right to buy the leased equipment at the end of the lease term under the same terms and conditions as offered by an unaffiliated third party. The disadvantage to using it is that a lessee may run the risk that a competitor may bid for the equipment either to push the price up or to acquire it for its own operations.

The Right to Upgrade Financing

At times, companies lease equipment, such as computer systems, that are likely to require upgrading during the lease term to ensure maximum performance by adding additional equipment or modifying the original equipment. Typically, an upgrade may not be done without the lessor's prior's prior written consent and, in some situations, it may be of such a nature, such as, for example, internal equipment modifications that have no standalone value, that no one other than the original lessor would consider financing it. In these situations, the incumbent lessor has absolute negotiating control over the upgrade financing and can charge the lessee more than the going market rate.

> **Recommendation:** To avoid having to accept whatever financing rate, your lessor offers for an equipment upgrade when no other lessor may be willing, or able, to finance an upgrade, insist on having an option to require equipment upgrade financing on some easy to assess terms. Although it may not be possible to have your upgrade financing at a predetermined fixed lease rate, ask for a rate that is to be determined in accordance with acceptable standards at the time of financing, such as the original lease rate adjusted for changes in prime rate.

If You Default You Will Lose Your Lease Options

Generally, a lease will provide that a lessee will forfeit their option exercise rights, if they are in default under the lease. For example, a lessee will lose their right to buy the equipment under a purchase option if the lease is terminated because of default on its part.

Designate the Law Governing the Lease

Typically, a lease will specify what jurisdiction's law will apply to the parties' rights and obligations. For example, it may provide that all actions on lease issues will be decided under the laws of New York State, regardless of whether the proceedings are instituted in a New York court. By doing this, the attorneys are able to draft the documents under the law they believe will give the fairest known outcome.

> **Recommendation:** As part of your lease negotiations, ask for the law in the state you operate out of to govern lease disputes.

The Interest Penalty for Late Payments

A lease agreement will often prescribe the interest rate that will be charged on any overdue payments, such as delinquent rent payments. This will eliminate disputes over late charges and will assist in assessing damages if a lawsuit arises.

> **Recommendation:** Require that your company receives written notice and, say, a 30-day period from the date of notice receipt, to correct any late payment before any interest on any overdue obligations starts to run.

The Lease Should Identify Where and How to Send Any Required Notifications and Payments

While leases usually provide that all required notifications and payments, such as loss notifications and rent payments, must be promptly made, they sometimes fail to identify exactly *where* they should be sent. As a result, payments or notifications could be misdirected and money or valuable time lost. The lease should, therefore, expressly state the appropriate mailing addresses.

In addition to specifying where payments and notifications must be sent, the lease should specify the notification and payment manner. For example, it may be agreed that a notice will be deemed given when it is deposited in a U.S. mailbox, sent by national overnight carrier, or sent by certified mail.

Summary

The lease document sets out the business arrangement that both the lessor and lessee have agreed to enter into—their rights and duties. You, of course, must carefully review it to ensure that it is written to cover all aspects that are important to your company as a lessee. This cannot be done without understanding each aspect of a typically lease contract and what negotiating leeway is fairly and reasonably available.

CHAPTER 10

Closing the Lease Financing

Overview

Once you have negotiated the terms and conditions of your lease agreement, it is time to have it put in final form and prepare for what is referred to as the lease *closing*. At the closing, all parties will sign the lease agreement and, in addition, fulfill any closing conditions identified or requested in accordance with the lease or other governing papers, such as the lessee delivering to the lessor any specified *collateral* documents requested. These collateral, or supplemental, documents range from those that essentially provide comfort on specified issues, such as opinions of counsel, to those that define critical supportive arrangements, such as guarantee agreements. All the collateral documents are an integral part of the finance closing. If a lessee, for example, is unable to provide any, the lessor has no obligation to provide the financing.

The leveraged lease closing is the most complex, because of the major added participant—the third-party equipment lender. Even though the actual leveraged lease agreement does not differ radically from that of a non-leveraged lease, additional supplemental closing documents are usually involved, such as a security and loan agreement to accommodate the loan arrangement requirements. Although a lessee will not be a party to, nor even see, many of the additional leveraged lease-related documents involved, they will likely be subject to the delays processing these documents may cause.

Although drafting the supplemental papers will be the responsibility of the transaction lawyers, the business people should understand the fundamental concepts involved so that the relevant papers can be meaningfully reviewed to ensure they accurately reflect the agreements reached. Also, understanding the purpose of the collateral documents will enable the business participants to more readily negotiate compromises when the lawyers reach impasses. And, that is the purpose of this chapter—to provide you with a closing document overview so that you know in advance what to expect and to enable you to assist when necessary to facilitate a smooth closing.

One final point before we begin. While this chapter provides a general working knowledge of the typical collateral lease documents, keep in mind that many transactions have their own unique aspects that must also be taken into account.

Legal Opinions

The Function of Legal Opinions

In large-ticket (multimillion dollar) and, at times, middle-market (typically less than one million U.S. dollars, but more than 250,000 U.S. dollars) lease transactions, legal opinions are typically required by lessors and, in some cases, by sophisticated lessees. Before going into the various opinions possible and what they might address, let us take a moment to go over what the practical value of such an opinion may be from a business and legal point of view. To begin with, it is important to understand what a legal opinion does not do. It does not guarantee that the conclusions expressed in the opinion are correct. Regardless of the quality of the lawyer's work in preparing the opinion, a court or administrative agency may interpret the law or facts differently—and their decision, not the legal opinion, will be controlling. A legal opinion, however, does provide the recipient with value:

- It provides the participants with a significant degree of comfort, because the lawyer's opinion usually will be correct.
- In drafting an opinion, the lawyer will need access to relevant information and, therefore, writing it may bring to light transaction trouble spots that can be corrected.
- If a court or agency disagrees with the opinion, having it may help show that the parties exercised due care in entering the transaction and may prevent the imposition of any penalties.

The problem with legal opinions is they are invariably qualified by, for example, stating a very specific set of facts or assumptions on which they are based. To the extent that the relevant facts are not properly conveyed to the lawyer providing the opinion or the assumptions are incorrect or faulty, the opinion may be of little value.

Recommendations:

- Although legal opinions often make the recipient feel secure on the issues covered, there are times when more certainty is required. For example, you may be concerned over whether a certain lease structure qualifies as a lease for federal income tax purposes, and you may be well advised to consider getting an Internal Revenue Service ruling on the issue.
- The *expertness* of the lawyer providing an opinion is a critical consideration, particularly when complex legal issues are involved. Therefore, if you need a legal opinion in a lease transaction, choose a lawyer with solid leasing or other relevant experience.

Opinion from a Lessee's Lawyer

The lessor will typically ask a lessee to have their attorney deliver a legal opinion on relevant legal issues. The opinion's goal is to provide the lessor with assurances that no legal issues exist that will undermine the lease transaction. Thus, a lessor will typically want a lessee's lawyer to opine whether:

- The lessee has been properly organized, is validly in existence, and is in good standing under the laws of their state of organization;
- The lessee has the authority to enter into the lease;
- The lessee has the ability to perform all of its lease obligations;
- All the lessee's lease commitments are legally binding;
- Any consents, such as those of the shareholders or lenders, are necessary and, if so, whether they have been obtained; and
- Any regulatory approvals, such as a state public utility commission, are necessary and, if so, whether all the proper action has been taken;

- There are any adverse pending or threatened court or administrative proceedings against the lessee and, if so, their probable outcome; and
- The lessee would violate any law, rule, or provision of any of its existing agreements by entering into the lease arrangement or complying with any of its terms.

Opinions from Lessor's Lawyer

To the Lessee

In certain situations, particularly in large-ticket underwritten leveraged lease transactions, your company, as a lessee, should consider obtaining an opinion from the lessor's lawyer concerning the lessor's legal ability to enter into and perform its obligations. That opinion should minimally confirm that the lessor is properly:

- Incorporated or organized, as the case may be, at the time the lease is signed; and
- Qualified to do business in the state where the equipment will be used to avoid, for example, any risk that the equipment could be attached by the state authorities for the nonpayment of any taxes that the lessor may owe.

To the Lender

In the case of a leveraged lease transaction, the equipment lender will typically request a written opinion from the lessor's lawyer on key issues relating to its loan arrangement with the lessor. This type of opinion generally covers the same issues as those covered in the opinion requested to be given to the lessee. For example, whether:

- The lessor is duly organized, validly existing, and in good standing in their state of organization;
- All the necessary transaction authorizations have been secured; and
- The lessor's obligations under the loan documents are fully enforceable;

- The lessor has good and marketable title to the equipment covered by the lease;
- The equipment is free and clear of any liens or encumbrances other than those of which the lender is aware;
- The lessor has not made any other lease assignments; and
- The lender has a free and unencumbered right to receive all payments, such as rent under the lease agreement.

Opinion from the Guarantor's Lawyer

In some situations, a third party will guarantee a lessee's lease obligations. For example, the parent company of a financially weak corporate lessee may be asked to guarantee the lease obligations as a condition to the lessor's lease commitment. In that case, the strength and viability of the guarantor's commitment is critical to the lessor and any nonrecourse equipment lender. To help confirm the guarantee's worth, a lessor will request a favorable opinion from the guarantor's lawyer on the applicable aspects, addressing legal issues that relate to the guarantor's ability to fulfill the guarantee. For example, the opinion may be required to state whether:

- The guarantor is duly organized, validly existing, and in good standing;
- Anything exists that could adversely affect the guarantee's quality, such as material litigation;
- The guarantee has been fully and properly authorized; and
- The guarantee is a legally enforceable obligation.

Opinion from the Vendor's Lawyer

Usually, the leased equipment's vendor is not asked to provide any legal opinion because they have only to deliver a clear title to the equipment, and an adequate bill of sale containing proper seller representations and warranties typically gives the necessary comfort. In certain situations, particularly if a substantial dollar amount of equipment is involved, a prospective lessor might ask the equipment vendor for their lawyer to provide a legal opinion confirming that the vendor has, upon equipment payment, delivered a clear title to the equipment.

Financial Reports and Information

The financial strength of every party to the lease transaction, such as the lessor, the lessee, and any third-party guarantor, can be a key factor in a lease financing and, therefore, it is important that reliable and up-to-date financial information be obtained. The degree of information necessary depends on the transaction's size—a lease of a 2,000 U.S. dollar office copier will not warrant the same degree of financial investigation that would be called for in the lease of a multimillion-dollar printing press.

Why Financial Information Is Necessary

Of the Lessor

The financial condition of a lessor is an important lessee consideration—a solid lessor contractual commitment to lease is worthless if they do not have funds available when the equipment, particularly if it is to be delivered in the future, arrives for lease. All too often a prospective lessee fails to check the lessor's financial condition, apparently assuming that a lessor always has adequate funds and, that, once the deal has been signed, there is nothing to be concerned about. This may not be true. A financially weak lessor may not have purchase funds available when the equipment is ready for lease. And, even if the equipment has been paid for and put on lease, there is a risk, although an unlikely one, that the lessor's creditors may attempt to seize the leased equipment as security for an unpaid obligation.

The availability of adequate funds for equipment purchase is of particular concern if a lease line of credit is involved, that is, when the lessor has committed to buy and lease many items of equipment to be delivered over a long period. Any lack of available lessor financing when equipment arrives could be a serious problem for a would-be lessee.

Of the Lessee

Similarly, a lessee's financial condition is a critical element in the lessor's decision as to whether to enter into a particular lease financing, particularly if a multimillion-dollar, long-term lease is involved. So, at all times, the lessor, particularly at the lease closing and when they must advance funds, will want to be assured that the lessee has the financial capability to meet all of its contractual obligations, including payment of rent, for the full lease term.

Of a Controlling Corporation or Entity

If the lessee is owned by another company, very often, a lessor will want to review the parent company's financial statements—even if the parent does not guarantee the lease obligations and regardless of the financial strength of the lessee. The weaker the financial condition of an owning company, the greater the possibility that it will drain the lessee's cash to solve any of its financial problems.

Of the Guarantor

If a potential lessee's financial condition is inadequate, as a condition of going forward with the financing, the lessor may ask for a transaction guarantee from a financially solid entity, such as a parent company or equipment vendor. In this event, the guarantor's financial strength is of primary importance and relevant financial information may be included in the closing.

Type of Financial Information Needed

Typically, the financial condition of a company can be adequately assessed in a review of its past and present financial statements, including profit and loss statements and balance sheets. A lessor may, particularly for smaller companies, also require bank and trade references to further verify the financial integrity of the company being reviewed. And, it may check, particularly in the case of smaller companies, with credit reporting services, such as Dunn and Bradstreet or Experian, to see if there is any adverse information on file.

At times, a lessor's financial review is preliminarily done prior to it issuing a lease proposal offer, but typically an in-depth review is not done until shortly after the lease award, particularly if the proposal offer is subject to the leasing company's credit committee approval. In any event, it is always done well in advance of starting the documentation negotiation.

A lessor may also ask that the financially reviewed entity, particularly if there is a long time between the review and the lease signing, bring its financial information up to the closing date. One of the most common ways a participant's financial picture is brought up to the transaction's closing date is to require the reviewed entity's financial officer to deliver a certificate at the closing presenting and updating relevant financial information since the last published financial statements. For example, if the most current financial statements reflect a company's condition as of June 15, 20XX, and the transaction does not close until September 25, 20XX, the certificate must essentially provide that as of the closing date, September 25, 20XX, there have been no materially adverse financial changes since the date of the latest financial statements, June 15, 20XX. Of course, it would be more comforting to get the company's independent accountants to issue the certificate, but this is generally not practical.

Corporate or Other Organizational Authorization Documents

When a corporation participates as a lessee in a large lease transaction, the lessor generally requires the delivery at lease closing of a certified copy of the corporation's board of directors' resolutions authorizing the transaction from the corporate secretary or assistant secretary. The typical lessee corporate resolution, for example, will state that the lessee has been duly authorized to enter into the transaction for the specified dollar amount and, that, an identified person has been authorized to execute the documents on behalf of the corporation. For other types of lessee entities, similar authorization documents or comfort may be required.

> **Recommendation:** While lessors and lenders usually require lessees to deliver appropriate board of directors' resolutions or other authorizing documents at a lease closing, lessees rarely ask for authorizing resolutions or other authorizing documents from the other parties. However, if your company, as a lessee, is dealing with corporate or other types of lessor participants or lenders not regularly engaged in leasing or lending, you should seriously consider making a similar request.

Guarantees

When a prospective lessee wants to lease more equipment than their credit capability justifies, they will be asked for additional credit support. Very often, the lessor will suggest that a financially strong third party be brought in to guarantee the lessee's obligations. The guarantee request may vary anywhere from a full guarantee of all the lease obligations to something significantly less.

The most favorable guarantee for a lessor is a full lessee lease guarantee, where the guarantor unconditionally obligates themselves to ensure the lessee's full and prompt performance of all the lease obligations, covenants, and conditions. For example, if the lessee fails to pay the rent, the lessor could go directly to the guarantor for payment. Under a partial guarantee, the guarantor may, for example, only be responsible for the repayment of 15 percent of the total lease payments. Partial guarantees may be acceptable to a lessor when the proposed transaction is financially attractive.

Proof of Insurance Documents

Frequently, the lease agreement will require that the lessee have personal injury and property damage insurance covering the leased equipment, insurance that will also cover the lessor. In these cases, the lessor will want the lessee to confirm that the insurance will be in effect when the equipment is accepted for lease. That confirmation will typically be required to be delivered at the lease closing and will take the form of a certificate of insurance from the lessee's insurance company stating that the necessary coverage will be in effect.

Equipment Purchase Agreements

Unless the equipment is already owned by the lessee, the lessor will have to purchase it from a third-party supplier. If the equipment is available at the time the lease is signed, and it is ready for lease acceptance, the lessor simply pays for it at that time of its acceptance for lease. It is not unusual, however, for a lessee to have entered into an equipment purchase contract with the equipment supplier well before the equipment is to be delivered and, if so, typically the right, but not the obligation, to purchase the equipment under the purchase agreement is assigned to the lessor.

> **Recommendation:** Any assignment of the right to purchase the equipment to a leasing company should be subject to the lessor fulfilling their lease commitment.

An Equipment Bill of Sale

A prospective lessor generally requires that the equipment seller deliver a bill of sale when they pay for the equipment. Typically, the bill of sale is a warranty bill of sale in which the seller not only transfers equipment title, but also warrants that they have delivered to the purchaser full legal and beneficial ownership to the equipment, free and clear of all liens, claims, and encumbrances. Such a bill of sale commonly has a seller representation that they have the lawful right and the appropriate authority to sell the equipment.

Waivers from Landowners or Mortgagees

Very often, equipment to be leased is to be located on real property leased from a third party or on property that is subject to a mortgage. In this case, statutory lien rights may exist that, for example, permit a landlord to attach any equipment on their land, including leased equipment, if its rent is not paid. Similarly, the holder of a mortgage on a lessee's building may, under a general mortgage claim right, be able to go after leased equipment located in the building. In these situations, the prospective lessor will typically require, as a closing document, a waiver from the landlord or mortgagee of any claim to the leased equipment.

Participation Agreements

A participation agreement, a closing document setting out the lease financing's structural terms and conditions, is frequently used in underwritten lease transactions, particularly leveraged lease transactions. The parties to such an agreement may include the lessee, the equity participants, the debt participants, and any trust established for the debt or equity participants. The participation agreement states the terms under which the debt participants must make their loans and the equity participants must make their equity investments. It also generally incorporates a method for substituting any defaulting participants.

The Owner's Trust Agreement

It is not unusual for a trust to be established for equity participants in a leveraged lease transaction, particularly if more than one equity participant is involved. The trust arrangement, referred to as an owner's trust, provides the equity participants with corporate-like liability protection and partnership-like income tax treatment and, thus, can be a desirable ownership vehicle.

To set up a trust, the equity participants enter into a trust agreement with an entity, such as a bank, that will act as the trustee referred to as the *owner trustee*. The agreement sets out in detail how, and to what extent, the trustee will act on behalf of the equity participants.

As a part of its trust obligations, the trustee will execute all relevant documents, including the lease, any participation agreement, the indenture, and any purchase agreement assignment, on behalf of each equity participant. The right, title, and interest in the equipment, the lease, any purchase agreement, and any purchase agreement assignment are collectively referred to as the trust estate, and legal title to the equipment is held in the owner trustee's name. The owner trustee is, however, only a figurehead owner, the beneficial interest in the trust estate residing with the equity participants. The equity participant's interests are represented by certificates, referred to as owner certificates, issued by the owner trustee.

A Lender's Trust Agreement

If the financing is structured as a leveraged lease, and there are more than one debt participants, they will typically act through a trust arrangement that enables them to receive favorable tax treatment and liability protection. The arrangement is typically set up through a trust indenture and mortgage agreement entered into between the equity participants and debt participants. A trust indenture and mortgage agreement defines the basic debt financing parameters and provides for issuing loan certificates that set out the debt repayment obligations. The agreement also grants a security interest to the lenders in the equipment and the lease while the loan is outstanding.

The debt trust structure is similar to the equity trust structure. The debt participants are represented by a trustee, referred to as the *loan trustee*, and it stands in the same position to the debt participants as does the owner trustee to the equity participants. As the lender's *watchdog*, the trustee can take any prescribed action that may be necessary to protect the debt participants' interests, such as foreclosing on the lease in case of default. As with a participation agreement, it will be one of the lease closing documents.

Using a Partnership Instead of a Trust Arrangement

At times, multiple equity or debt participants find it undesirable or impractical to act through a trust arrangement. In that case, they frequently use instead a partnership structure. Here, the *lessor* or *lender*, as the case may be, is the partnership, with the equity or debt participants as partners in the partnership. It is usually advisable for a formal partnership agreement to be entered into that defines each partner's rights and obligations. The agreement will be a part of the lease closing on the lessor's side.

The Underwriter's Fee Agreement

In underwritten transactions, the lease underwriter will be responsible for bringing together the equity participants, the lessee, and, if the transaction is leveraged, the debt participants. For their services, the underwriter will be entitled to a fee, typically varying with each transaction and each underwriter, payable by the equity participants. To protect themself and prevent later misunderstandings as to the payment terms, the underwriter may ask that the equity participants enter into a formal fee agreement clearly defining the fee arrangement, which will also be included as a closing document on the lessor's side.

Summary

The ancillary documents that accompany the closing of a lease transaction are often overlooked until the last minute, frequently being given little thought because of their supplemental nature. These documents, however, can give rise to problems, concerns, or issues that can prevent or unduly delay a lease transaction closing. Understanding what they are, and how they work, will facilitate avoiding costly closing issues.

Appendix

Definitions of Leasing Terms

Sample Request for Bids Letter

Suggested Additional Reference and Research Material:

Books:

The Handbook of Equipment Leasing, by Shawn D. Halladay and Sudhir P. Amenbal

Equipment Leasing, by Frank Fabozzi

Equipment Leasing – Leveraged Leasing, various authors, published by the Practicing Law Institute

The Complete Handbook of Equipment Leasing, Second Edition, 2015, Richard M. Contino, Esq., published by York House Press

Business Resources:

First Lease Advisors (https://firstleaseadvisors.com)

Equipment Leasing and Financing Industry Contacts:

Equipment Leasing and Finance Association (https://elfaonline.org/)

Lease Evaluation and Pricing Consultants:

Ivory Consulting Corporation, Walnut Creek, California (https://ivorycc.com/)

Fairfield Capital Group, LLC (https://fairfieldcapital.net)

Legal Sources:

Martindale Hubble (https://martindale.com)

Contino + Partners (https://continopartners.com)

Equipment Lease Terminology—The Definitions

When entering into a leasing transaction, you may encounter unfamiliar terms that have developed along with the leasing industry. This following is a listing of various terms used in the leasing industry and their definitions according to their industry usage.

- **Acceptance certificate:** A document in which a lessee acknowledges that certain specified equipment is acceptable for lease. Generally used in transactions where the parties enter into the lease document well in advance of the equipment's delivery date, it serves to notify the lessor that the equipment has been delivered, inspected, and accepted for lease as of a specified date. The typical form requires the lessee to list certain pertinent information, including the equipment manufacturer, purchase price, serial number, and location.

- **Acceptance supplement:** The same as an acceptance certificate.

- **Advance rental:** Any payment in the form of rent made before the start of the lease term. The term is also sometimes used to describe a rental payment arrangement in which the lessee pays all rentals, on a per period basis, at the start of each rental payment period. For example, a quarterly, in advance, rental program requires the lessee to pay one-fourth of the annual rental at the start of each consecutive three-month period during the lease term.

- **Balloon payment:** Commonly found in mortgage financings, a balloon payment is a final payment that is larger than the periodic term payments. Usually, it results because the debt has not been fully amortized during the repayment period. For example, a one-year financing arrangement providing for interest-only monthly payments during the year, with the principal plus the last interest payment due on the final payment date, is said to have a *balloon payment* or simply a *balloon* due at the end of the term.

- **Bareboat charter party**: A net financial lease relating to vessels. Also sometimes referred to simply as a *bareboat charter*. See Net lease.
- **Base lease term:** The primary period that the lessee is entitled to use the leased equipment, without regard to any interim or renewal lease terms. The base lease term of a five-year lease is five years.
- **Base rental:** The rental that the lessee must pay during the base, sometimes called primary, lease term.
- **Beneficial interest holder:** Refers to a beneficial, as opposed to legal title, owner. For example, when a trust has been created by the equity participants to act as the lessor, the equity participants are deemed the beneficial interest holders. They hold interests in the trust that has title to the equipment.
- **Bond:** An instrument that represents a long-term debt obligation. The debt instruments, sometimes referred to as loan certificates, issued in a leveraged lease transaction, are referred to as bonds or notes.
- **Book reporting:** The reporting of income or loss for financial as opposed to tax purposes on the financial records of a corporation or other reporting entity.
- **Book residual value:** An estimate of the equipment's residual value that a lessor uses, or *books*, to calculate its economic return on a lease transaction.
- **Broker:** A person or entity who, for compensation, arranges lease transactions for another's account. A broker is also referred to as a syndicator or underwriter.
- **Call:** The right a lessee may have to buy specified leased equipment for a predetermined fixed price, usually expressed as a percentage of original cost. If provided, such an option commonly does not become exercisable until the end of the lease term, and it lapses if the lessee fails to give the lessor timely notice of its intention to exercise it. For example, a lessee may have a right to buy equipment at the end of the lease term for 30 percent of the original cost, notice of intention

to exercise the option to be given not less than 90 days before the lease term's end.

- **Cash flow:** In a lease transaction, the amount of cash a lease generates for a lessor.
- **Casualty value:** A predetermined amount of money that a lessee guarantees the lessor will receive in the event of an equipment casualty loss during the lease term. Generally, expressed as a percentage of the original cost, the value varies according to the point in time during the lease term that the loss occurs. It is also referred to as a *stipulated loss value*.
- **Certificate of delivery and acceptance**: The same as acceptance certificate.
- **Charter party:** A document that provides for the lease (charter) of a vessel or vessels. While the format is basically the same as any other lease, there are certain additions and modifications reflecting the requirements dictated by a vessel transaction.
- **Charterer:** The lessee of a vessel.
- **Chattel mortgage:** A mortgage relating to personal property. Thus, a mortgage on equipment is a chattel mortgage.
- **Collateral:** Assets used as security for the repayment of a debt obligation. In a typical leveraged lease, the lender's collateral is the leased equipment.
- **Commencement date:** The date the base, or primary, lease term begins.
- **Commission agreement:** An agreement between a lease broker and a prospective equity participant providing for the payment of a fee to the broker for services in arranging a lease transaction.
- **Commitment fee:** Compensation paid to a lender in return for an agreement to make a future loan or to a lessor for its commitment to lease equipment to a lessee in the future.
- **Conditional sale agreement.** A contract, also referred to as CSA, that provides for the time financing of asset purchases. The seller typically retains title to (but in any event maintains a security interest in) the asset until the buyer fulfills all spec-

ified conditions, such as installment payments. At that time, the title, if retained, automatically vests in the buyer (or, in the case of an existing security interest, is subject to release).

- **Cost of money:** Commonly, the cost that a lessor incurs to borrow money. This includes the interest rate and any additional costs related to such borrowing, such as fees or compensating balances. In pricing a lease transaction, a lessor factors this cost into the lessee's lease payment computation.

- **Cost-to-customer:** The simple interest rate on a lease transaction, often called simply the *c2c*.

- **Debt participant:** A long-term lender in a leveraged lease transaction. Frequently, these transactions have more than one debt participant.

- **Debt service:** The aggregate periodic repayment amount, including principal and interest, due on a loan.

- **Default:** In a lease transaction, when a party breaches certain material lease obligations.

- **Deficiency guarantee**: A guarantee given to a lessor by a third party, such as an equipment vendor or manufacturer, to induce a lessor to enter into a lease that they would not otherwise enter into usually because the prospective lessee may be a poor credit risk, or because the future value of equipment may be highly speculative. For example, a deficiency guarantor may agree to pay the lessor for any shortfall below a designated amount, say 20 percent of the original cost, incurred when the equipment is sold at the end of the lease.

- **Delivery and acceptance certificate:** The same as an acceptance certificate.

- **Depreciation indemnity:** A tax indemnification given by a lessee against the lessor's loss of anticipated depreciation tax benefits on leased equipment.

- **Discounted cash flow analysis:** The process of determining the present value of future cash flows.

- **Equipment certificate of acceptance:** The same as an acceptance certificate.

- **Equity participant:** The equity investor in a leveraged lease. Frequently, a leveraged lease transaction has more than one equity participant, who jointly own and lease the equipment. An equity participant is also sometimes referred to as an *owner participant*.
- **Event of default:** An event that provides the basis for the declaration of a default. For example, the nonpayment of rent under a lease agreement is typically prescribed as an event of default that gives the lessor the right to declare the lease in default and to pursue permitted remedies, such as terminating the lease and reclaiming the equipment.
- **Fair market purchase value:** An asset's value as determined in the open market in an arm's length transaction (one in which there is a willing buyer and a willing seller, under no compulsion to act) under normal selling conditions. It is also referred to simply as the asset's *fair market value*.
- **Fair market rental value:** The rental rate that an asset would command in the open market in an arm's length transaction (one in which there is a willing lessee and a willing lessor, under no compulsion to act) under normal renting conditions. It is also referred to simply as the asset's *fair rental value*.
- **FASB:** The Financial Accounting Standards Board, the accounting profession's guideline setting authority.
- **FAS Statement No. 13, Accounting for Leases:** FAS No. 13 sets out the standards for financial lease accounting for lessors and lessees.
- **Finance lease:** The same as a full payout lease.
- **Financing agreement:** An agreement commonly entered into by the principal parties to a leveraged lease before equipment delivery. The agreement identifies each party's obligation to the transaction and any conditions that must be satisfied before the obligations are fixed. Typically, it will involve the debt and equity participants, their representatives, and the lessee. It is also referred to as a *participation agreement*.
- **Floating rental rate:** A form of periodic rental payments that change or *float* upward and downward over a lease's term with

changes in a specified interest rate. Frequently, a designated bank's prime rate is the measuring interest rate.

- **Full payout lease:** A form of lease that will provide the lessor with a cash flow generally sufficient to return their equipment investment; pay the principal, interest, and other financing costs on related debt; cover its related sales and administration expenses; and generate a profit. The cash flow is determined from the rental payments, the ownership tax benefits, and the equipment residual value. The lessee typically has the right to use the leased equipment for most of its actual useful life.

- **Gross income tax:** A tax imposed by a state or local taxing authority on gross income generated from sources within its jurisdiction. The tax is deductible by the taxpayer for federal income tax purposes.

- **Grossing up:** A concept that any reimbursement for a monetary loss will include sufficient additional monies so that the after-tax amount will equal the loss. The recipient is said to be made whole for their loss because the amount paid must take into account any taxes they will have to pay as a result of the receipt of the payments from the payor.

- **Guaranteed residual value:** An arrangement in which, for example, a broker or equipment manufacturer guarantees that a lessor will receive not less than a certain amount for specified equipment when it is disposed of at the end of the lease term. It is also sometimes referred to simply as a *guaranteed residual*.

- **Guideline lease:** A leveraged lease that meets with IRS's lease guidelines such as set out in Revenue Procedures 2001-28 and 2001-29, as updated. While the guidelines specifically address only private ruling requests, generally a guideline lease should qualify as a true lease for federal income tax purposes.

- **Half-year convention:** A concept under the income tax rules for depreciating equipment under which all equipment placed in service during a tax year is treated as having been placed in service at the mid-point of that year, regardless of when during the year it was in fact placed in service.

- **Hell or high-water clause**: A lease provision that commits a lessee to pay the rent unconditionally. The lessee waives any right that exists or may arise to withhold any rent from the lessor or any assignee of the lessor for any reason whatsoever, including any setoff, counterclaim, recoupment, or defense.
- **High-low rental:** A rental structure in which the rent payments are reduced from a higher to a lower rate at a prescribed point in the lease term.
- **Implicit lease rate:** The annual interest rate that, when applied to the lease rental payments, will discount those payments to an amount equal to the cost of the equipment leased.
- **Indemnity agreement:** A contract in which one party commits to insure another party against anticipated and specified losses.
- **Indenture:** In a leveraged lease transaction, an agreement entered into by an owner trustee (the lessor's representative) and an indenture trustee (the lender's representative) in which the owner trustee grants a lien on the leased equipment, the lease rents, and other lessor contract rights as security for repayment of the outstanding equipment loan. It is also referred to as an indenture trust.
- **Indenture trustee:** The representative of the lenders where, in a leveraged lease transaction, the debt is provided through a trust arrangement. As the lender's representative, the indenture trustee may, for example, have to file and maintain a security interest in the leased equipment, receive rentals from the lessee, pay out the proper amounts to the lenders and the lessor, and take certain action to protect the outstanding loan in the event of a loan default.
- **Installment sale:** A sale in which the purchase price is paid in an agreed-upon number of installment payments over an agreed-upon period. Typically, the title to what is sold does not transfer to the purchaser until, and only when, the last installment has been paid.

- **Institutional investors:** Institutions that invest in lease transactions. They can be, for example, insurance companies, pension funds, banks, or trusts.
- **Insured value:** The same as casualty value.
- **Interim lease rental:** The equipment rental due for the interim lease term. Typically, for each day during the interim lease term, a lessee must pay as interim lease rent an amount equal to the daily equivalent of the primary lease term rent. In a leveraged lease transaction, the lease sometimes instead permits the lessee to pay an amount equal to the daily equivalent of the long-term debt interest.
- **Interim lease term:** The lease term period between the lessee's acceptance of the equipment for lease and the beginning of the primary, or base, lease term.
- **Investment tax credit (ITC):** A credit allowed against federal income tax liability that can be claimed by a taxpayer for certain *Section 38 property* acquired and placed in service by a taxpayer during a tax year. Under the federal tax laws, ITC is generally not available, other than for certain energy equipment.
- **ITC indemnity:** A type of indemnification in which the lessee commits to reimburse the lessor for any financial loss incurred through the loss of, or inability to claim, any or all of the anticipated ITC. If the lessor has *passed through* the ITC to the lessee, the lessor may have to give the indemnity.
- **ITC *pass-through*:** An election made by the lessor to treat, for ITC purposes, the lessee as the owner of the leased equipment. After the election, a lessee can claim the ITC on the equipment covered by the election.
- **Layoff:** The sale by a lessor of their interest in the lease agreement, including the ownership of the leased equipment and the right to receive the rent payments.
- **Lease agreement:** A contract in which an equipment owner, the lessor, transfers the equipment's use, subject to the specified terms and conditions, to another, the lessee, for a prescribed period and rental rate.

- **Lease line:** A present commitment by a lessor to lease specified equipment to be delivered in the future. A lease line can cover a variety of types of equipment, at varying rental rates and lease terms. It is also referred to as a lease line of credit.
- **Lease underwriting:** The process in which a lease broker arranges a lease transaction for the account of third parties, a prospective lessor, and a prospective lessee. This can be on a best efforts basis or on a firm commitment basis. In a best efforts underwriting, the broker only offers to attempt diligently to arrange the financing on certain proposed terms. In a firm commitment underwriting, the broker in effect guarantees to arrange the financing as proposed.
- **Lessee:** The user of equipment that is the subject of a lease agreement.
- **Lessor:** The owner of equipment that is the subject of a lease agreement.
- **Level payments:** Payments that are the same for each payment period during the payment term. Frequently, rent and debt service payments are paid in level payments over the payment period.
- **Leveraged lease:** A lease in which a portion, generally 60 to 80 percent of the equipment acquisition cost is borrowed from a bank or other lending institution, with the lessor paying the balance. The debt is commonly on a nonrecourse basis, and the rental payments are usually sufficient to cover the loan debt service.
- **Limited-use property:** Leased property that will be economically usable only by the lessee, or a member of the lessee group, at the lease term's end because, for example, of its immobility or unique aspects. The IRS will not rule that a lease is a true lease where the leased equipment is limited use property.
- **Loan certificate:** A certificate that evidences a debt obligation.
- **Loan participant:** A debt participant.

- **Low-high rental:** A rental structure in which the rent payments are increased from a lower to a higher rate at a prescribed point in the lease term.
- **Management agreement**: A contract in which one party agrees to manage a lease transaction during its term, including, for example, rental payment processing and equipment disposal.
- **Management fee:** A fee that a lease transaction manager receives for services performed under a management agreement.
- **Master lease agreement:** A lease agreement designed to permit future equipment not contemplated when the lease is executed to be added to the lease later. The document is set up in two parts. The main body contains the general, or boilerplate, provisions, such as the maintenance and indemnification provisions. An annex, or schedule, contains the type of items that usually vary with a transaction, such as rental rates and options.
- **Mid-quarter convention:** A concept under the income tax rules for depreciating equipment in which all equipment placed in service during a quarter of a tax year is treated as placed in service at the mid-point of such quarter, regardless of when it was in fact placed in service during the quarter.
- **Modified Accelerated Cost Recovery System (MACRS):** A method prescribed for depreciating assets that was introduced by the 1986 TRA. It applies to most equipment placed in service after 1986.
- **Mortgage:** An arrangement whereby a lender (mortgagee) acquires a lien on property owned by a taxpayer (mortgagor) as security for the loan repayment. Once the debt obligation has been fully satisfied, the mortgage lien is terminated.
- **Negative spread:** The amount by which a value is below a certain prescribed amount. Generally, in a leveraged lease, a negative spread is the amount by which the transaction's simple interest rate is below the leveraged debt interest rate.

- **Net lease:** A lease arrangement in which the lessee is responsible for paying all costs, such as maintenance, certain taxes, and insurance, related to using the leased equipment, in addition to the rental payments. Typically, finance leases are net leases.
- **Nonpayout lease:** A lease arrangement that does not, over the primary term of the lease, generate enough cash flow to return substantially all the lessor's investment, debt financing costs, and sales and administration expenses.
- **Non-recourse debt financing:** A loan as to which the lender agrees to look solely to the lessee, the lease rents, and the leased equipment for the loan's repayment. As security for the loan repayment, the lender receives an assignment of the lessor's rights under the lease agreement and a grant of a first lien on the equipment. Although the lessor has no obligation to repay the debt in the event of a lessee default, their equity investment in the equipment is usually subordinated to the lender's rights.
- **Non-utilization fee:** A fee that a lessor may impose in return for their present commitment to buy and lease specified equipment in the future. The fee is generally expressed as a percentage of the aggregate unused portion of the initial dollar commitment, for example, 1 percent of the unused balance of a one million U.S. dollar lease line of credit. Thus, if all the commitment is used, no fee is payable.
- **Operating lease:** A form of lease arrangement in which the lessor generally commits to provide certain additional equipment related services, other than the straight financing, such as maintenance, repairs, or technical advice. Generally, operating leases are non-payout in nature. The term also refers to a lease classification under FAS 13.
- **Option:** A contractual right that can be exercised under the granting terms. For example, a fair market value purchase option in a lease is the right to buy the equipment covered by it for its fair market value.

- **Packager**: A person or entity who arranges a lease transaction for third parties. Also referred to as an underwriter, syndicator, or sometimes, a broker.
- **Participation agreement:** The same as a financing agreement.
- **Payout lease:** The same as a full payout lease.
- **Personal property:** The same as Section 38 property. Equipment is considered personal property, but real estate is not so considered.
- **Portfolio lease:** The term commonly refers to a lease that is entered into by a *professional* lessor for their own account and investment.
- **Present value:** The term refers to the present worth of a future stream of payments calculated by discounting the future payments at a desired interest rate.
- **Primary lease term:** The same as base lease term.
- **Private letter ruling**: A written opinion that the IRS issues in response to a taxpayer's request. The letter sets out IRS's position on the tax treatment of a proposed transaction. In leveraged lease transactions, for the IRS to issue a favorable private letter ruling, the request must comply with the IRS Guidelines.
- **Progress payments:** Payments that may be required by an equipment manufacturer or builder during the construction period toward the purchase price. Frequently required for costly equipment with a long construction period, the payments are designed to lessen the manufacturer's or builder's need to tie up their own funds during construction.
- **Purchase option:** The right to buy agreed-upon equipment at the times and the amounts specified in the option. Frequently, these options, if specified in a lease, are only exercisable at the end of the primary lease term, although they sometimes can be exercised during the primary lease term or at the end of any renewal term.
- **Put:** A right that a lessor may have to sell specified leased equipment to the lessee at a fixed price at the end of the initial

lease term. It is usually imposed to protect the lessor's residual value assumption.

- **Recourse debt financing:** A loan under which the lender may look to the general credit of the lessor, in addition to the lessee and the equipment, for repayment of any outstanding loan obligation. The lender is said to have a *recourse* against the lessor.
- **Renewal option:** An option frequently given to a lessee to renew the lease term for a specified rental and period.
- **Residual sharing:** A compensation technique sometimes used by syndicators for arranging a lease transaction. Under this, the equity participants must pay a predetermined percentage of what the equipment is sold for at the end of the lease. For example, a syndicator may get 50 percent of any amount realized exceeding 20 percent of the equipment's original cost on sale.
- **Residual value:** The value of leased equipment at the end of the lease term.
- **Right of first refusal:** The right of the lessee to buy the leased equipment, or renew the lease, at the end of the lease term, for any amount equal to that offered by an unaffiliated third party.
- **Sale-leaseback:** An arrangement in which an equipment buyer buys equipment for the purpose of leasing it back to the seller.
- **Sales tax:** A tax imposed on selling equipment, similar to any other sales tax on property sold.
- **Sales-type lease:** A classification for a particular type of lease prescribed under the lease accounting guidelines that the FASB set out in FAS 13, applicable to lessors.
- **Salvage value:** The amount, estimated for federal income tax purposes, that an asset is expected to be worth at the end of its useful life.
- **Section 38 property:** Tangible personal property and certain other tangible property, as defined by Internal Revenue Code, Section 38.

- **Security agreement:** An agreement that evidences an assignment by the lessor to the lender, as security for the equipment loan, of the lessor's rights under the lease agreement and a granting of a security interest in the leased equipment.
- **Sinking fund:** A fund frequently established in leveraged lease transactions by the lessor to accumulate funds to pay for future taxes.
- **Sinking fund rate:** The interest rate that a sinking fund is deemed to earn on accumulated funds.
- **Special purpose equipment:** The same as limited use property.
- **Spread:** The difference between two values. In lease transactions, the term is generally used to describe the difference between the lease interest rate and the interest rate on the debt.
- **Stipulated loss value:** The same as casualty value.
- **Sublease:** The re-lease by a lessee of equipment that is on lease to the lessee.
- **Take or pay contract:** An agreement in which one party commits to buy an agreed-upon quantity of goods or material from another at a predetermined price. If the goods or materials are not bought, the party making the purchase commitment must pay the party an amount of money equal to the cost of goods or materials it had committed to buy. For example, a public utility can agree to buy 100 tons of coal annually from a mining company, and if it does not buy this amount in any year, it will pay an amount of money equal to its sale price.
- **Tax lease:** The same as a true lease.
- **Tax Reform Act (TRA):** The 1986 TRA, a federal income tax act.
- **Termination option:** An option entitling a lessee to terminate the lease during the lease term for a predetermined value, termination value, if the equipment becomes obsolete or surplus to the lessee's needs. The lessor usually requires the lessee to sell the equipment to an unaffiliated third party, and the lessee

must pay the lessor any amount by which the sale proceeds are less than the termination value. Typically, any excess sales proceeds go to the lessor.

- **Termination value:** The amount that the lessee must pay the lessor if they exercise a lease termination option. Typically, the termination value is set as of each rental payment period and is generally expressed as a percentage of equipment cost. For example, the lessee may be permitted to terminate the lease at the end of the third year of a seven-year lease for an amount equal to 60 percent of cost.
- **Time sale:** An installment sale.
- **Total earnings:** The amount by which the aggregate rentals due the lessor over the entire lease term exceed the total equipment costs, including equity investment and debt financing costs. This concept does not consider the time value of money.
- **Transition rules:** Statutory rules enacted when there is a change in the tax laws. The transition rules allow certain transactions to be exempted from the law change. For example, transition rules permitted ITC to be claimed on certain equipment placed in service after 1985.
- **True lease:** An arrangement that qualifies for lease treatment for federal income tax purposes. Under a true lease, the lessee may deduct rental payments, and the lessor may claim the tax benefits accruing to an equipment owner.
- **Trust:** An arrangement in which property is held by one party for the benefit of another. It is frequently used in leveraged lease transactions.
- **Trust certificate:** A trust document issued on behalf of a trust to evidence the beneficial ownership in the trust estate.
- **Trustee:** The person or entity appointed, or designated, to carry out a trust's terms. In leveraged lease transactions, the trustee is generally a bank or trust company.
- **Trustee fees:** Fees payable to a trustee as compensation for services performed.
- **Trustor:** An individual or entity who causes the creation of a trust and for whose benefit it is established.

- **Unleveraged lease:** A lease in which the lessor puts up 100 percent of the equipment's acquisition cost from its own funds.
- **Use tax:** A tax imposed upon the use, storage, or consumption of tangible personal property within a taxing jurisdiction. For example, in most states, a lessor purchasing equipment has the option of paying an upfront sales tax equal to a specified percentage of the equipment's purchase price or a use tax equal to a specified percentage of lease rents under the equipment's lease.
- **Useful life:** Commonly, the economic usable life of an asset.
- **Vendor:** A seller of property. Commonly, the manufacturer or distributor of equipment.
- **Vendor program:** A program in which an equipment lessor provides a lease financing service to customers of an equipment manufacturer.

Sample Request for Bids Letter

A Formal Request for Quotes Letter

Request for Quotations
TO
Lease Equipment
April 12, 20 __

SunTime Corporation is issuing this Request For Quotations (RFQ) to obtain equipment lease bids from perspective lessors. This RFQ is not an offer to contract. SunTime Corporation will not be obligated to lease the specified equipment until a mutually satisfactory written lease has been executed by all parties.

A. *Proposal Request - General*

In accordance with the terms and conditions specified below, SunTime Corporation wishes to receive proposals from equipment leasing companies (Lessors) to provide lease financing for certain data processing equipment.

In the evaluation of each proposal, SunTime Corporation will rely on all written and verbal representations made by each prospective Lessor and each representation will be incorporated into any and all formal agreements between the parties.

No Lessor receiving this RFQ is authorized to act for, or on behalf of, SunTime Corporation prior to the receipt of written acceptance by SunTime Corporation of a satisfactory lease proposal and then only in accordance with the specific terms, if any, of the acceptance.

B. *Proposal Guidelines*

1. Your proposal must be submitted in writing and follow the guidelines in this RFQ. If it does not, it will be rejected.
2. All RFQ requirements must be addressed. Specifically identify any requirements that cannot be satisfied.
3. If you can offer any additional benefits not requested in this RFQ, identify them as "Additional Benefits" and state them in a separate section at the end of your proposal.

4. You must notify SunTime Corporation no later than the Lessor Proposal Intent Notification date specified in the Timetable below if you intend to submit a proposal in response to this RFQ.

5. SunTime Corporation may, without liability and in its sole discretion, amend or rescind this RFQ prior to the lease award. In such event each Lessor offering to submit a proposal will be supplied, as the case may be, with an RFQ amendment or a notification of our intent not to proceed.

6. Your proposal will be considered confidential and none of the contents will be disclosed to a competing Lessor.

7. You shall be responsible for all costs incurred in connection with the preparation of your proposal and any contract(s) in response to this RFQ.

8. Your proposal must be signed by a duly authorized representative of your company.

9. Your proposal must be submitted in triplicate and remain in effect at least until the Lessor Proposal Commitment Cut-off date specified in the Timetable below.

10. Your proposal should be accompanied by (a) a copy of your most recent annual report or financial statements or appropriate bank references with account officer name and telephone number, (b) a description of any material litigation in which you are presently involved, and (c) a statement of any potential conflict of interest, and plan to avoid it, as a result of an award.

11. SunTime Corporation intends to announce its award decision no later than the Award Announcement date specified in the Timetable below.

12. Any questions concerning this RFQ, should sent in writing to:

SunTime Corporation

1823 Third Avenue

New York, New York 11020

Attn. John Peterson

Telephone Number: (212) 754-2367

Any questions and answers which we feel would be of assistance to all Lessors submitting proposals, will be promptly distributed to each.

13. SunTime Corporation may enter simultaneously in negotiations with more than one Lessor and make an award to one or more without prior notification to others we are negotiating with.

14. Any information supplied to you in this RFQ by SunTime Corporation or otherwise by any representative in connection with this RFQ is confidential and may not be disclosed or used except in connection with the preparation of your proposal. If you must release any such information to any person or entity for the purpose of preparing your proposal, you must obtain an agreement prior to releasing the information that it will be treated as confidential by such person or entity and will not be disclosed except in connection with the preparation of your proposal.

15. If you are a selected Lessor, prior to our making the award you will be supplied with a copy of our form lease document(s) for your review. Your response to the acceptability of the document provisions, with exceptions noted in writing, will be a condition precedent to any award.

C. *Equipment Lease Requirements*

1. Equipment Description, Cost and Trade-In

a. The equipment will consist of electronic data processing equipment (Equipment) acquired from the following designated vendor(s):

Vendor	Equipment Description	Cost
StarByte Computer Corp.	(1) Model 423 Computer	$1,850,000
Buffalo, NY	(7) Model 3 Remote Ctrs.	350,000
Micro Tech, Inc. New York, NY	Material Tracking System	150,000
	Installation:	120,000
	Total:	$2,470,000

(i) The final cost of the Equipment may vary as much as + (10)% or - (20)%, and your financing offer must permit this leeway without penalty.

b. If you can provide more advantageous financing by supplying equipment you own, have access to, or can acquire through volume discount arrangements with a vendor, please provide the specifics in the Additional Benefits section. If you intend to offer to provide any used equipment, the serial number(s), current location(s) and owner(s) must be stated in your proposal.

(i) Any equipment you offer to supply must be delivered to SunTime Corporation at 937 Secour Drive, Buffalo, New York 11342 no later than the Anticipated Equipment Delivery Date specified in the time table in Section D below and ready for acceptance no later than the specified Anticipated Equipment Acceptance Date. You must provide a firm delivery date commitment with contractual assurances and remedies for failure to meet such date, which should be stated in your proposal.

c. The Equipment will replace equipment under an existing lease of computer equipment and SunTime Corporation would like you to propose an additional financing arrangement which would incorporate the buy-out (pre-payment) of that lease. The specifics of the existing lease are as follows:

Lessor: AmerLease Corp.

Lease Term: 7 Years

Lease Start Date: March 1, 20__

Lease Ending Date: February 28, 20__

Monthly Rent: $21,324, in advance

Lease Termination Amount as of August 31, 20__: $397,000

Equipment: StarByte XTRA Material Tracking Computer System

Original Equipment Cost: $1,253,000

Purchase Option: Fair Market

(i) If you can provide any other arrangement that would be beneficial, such as subleasing the existing equipment to another lessee, please so indicate.

2. Estimated Delivery and Acceptance Date

It is anticipated that the Equipment will be delivered and accepted for lease no later than the anticipated delivery and acceptance date(s) specified in the timetable below.

3. Equipment Payment

The Equipment must be paid for by Lessor no later than thrifty (30) days following acceptance for lease

4. Equipment Location

The Equipment will initially be accepted for lease at our manufacturing plant located at 937 Secour Drive, Buffalo, New York. We must have the right to move the equipment to any location in the United States without the prior consent of Lessor, but upon providing thirty (30) days prior written notice.

5. Primary Lease Term

Your proposal must provide offers to lease the Equipment for Primary Lease Terms of five (5) and seven (7) years.

The Primary Lease Terms must run from the later of the Equipment acceptance for lease or payment by Lessor for the Equipment.

6. Primary Term Rents

Rent payments must be quoted on a monthly, in advance, and quarterly, in arrears, basis.

The rent payments must be expressed as a percentage of Equipment Cost and be on a consecutive, level basis. The nominal lease interest rate must be provided for each rent quote.

SunTime Corporation shall not be obligated for payment of rent until the Equipment vendor has been paid in full.

7. Interim Lease Term

No Interim Lease Term will be permitted that Requires payment of interim rent.

8. Interim Rents

No Interim Lease Term rent payments will acceptable.

9. Options

a. SunTime Corporation must have the option to renew the term of the lease year to year for a total of three (3) years, on a fair market value basis. Offers providing for a fixed-price renewal will also be considered. Any fixed price offers should be included in an "Additional Benefits" section at the end of the Lessor's proposal.

b. Lessee must have the right to purchase the Equipment at the end of the Primary Lease Term and each Renewal Term for its then fair market value. Offers providing for the right to purchase for a fixed percentage of Equipment Cost will be given favorable consideration and should be included in an "Additional Benefits" section at the end of the Lessor's offer.

c. SunTime Corporation must have the right, beginning as of the end of the first year of the Primary Lease Term, to terminate the Lease prior to the end of the Primary Lease Term, or any Renewal Term, in the event the Equipment becomes obsolete of surplus to SunTime Corporation's needs.

   (i) In the event of an early termination, SunTime Corporation shall have the right to arrange for the sale or re-lease of the Equipment. Any proceeds from the sale, or anticipated proceeds from the lease, of the Equipment shall reduce any termination penalty payment required.

   (ii) A schedule of early termination values must be included with your proposal.

d. SunTime Corporation must have the right to upgrade the Equipment, by adding equipment or replacing components, at any time during the term of the lease and Lessor must provide financing for such upgrade for a term coterminous with the term remaining during the upgrade period at a financing rate which will not exceed Lessor's transaction nominal after-tax yield.

10. Insurance

The Equipment shall be self-insured.

11. Casualty Value Schedule

A schedule of casualty values, expressed as a percentage of Equipment Cost, for both the Primary Lease Term and any Renewal Term(s) must be submitted with your proposal.

12. Transaction Fees

Lessee will not pay financing commitment or non-utilization fees.

13. Single Source Preference

Preference will be given to Lessors who intend to provide 100% of the funds necessary to purchase the Equipment over those who intend to leverage the purchase with third-party debt. Your proposal must disclose your intent.

(a) In the event you determine it would be advantageous to propose a leveraged lease financing structure, it should be submitted assuming a long-term debt interest rate of 6.75% per annum. In addition, the following terms will apply:

(i) Our investment banker, Chicago First Corporation, will be responsible for securing the third-party leveraged lease debt at a rate satisfactory to SunTime Corporation, within our sole discretion.

(ii) You must provide assurance that the lease will qualify as a true lease for Federal income tax purposes under the current tax rules and guidelines.

(iii) You must state whether your proposal is on a best efforts or firm basis; preference will be given to those on a firm basis.

(iv) At the time of submission of your proposal you must be prepared to identify all lease participants (with contact name and telephone number), including each identified equity and debt participant, so they may be called immediately for verification in the event you are the successful bidder.

14. Broker Disclosure

We will give a preference to lease offers from principal funding sources who do not intend to re-sell or broker the transaction. In the event that you do not intend to act as a principal and purchase the equipment for your own account, you must disclose that in your proposal.

15. Expenses

Lessor shall be responsible for payment of all fees and expenses of the transaction, other than Lessee's own direct legal fees in connection with documenting the lease transaction, including fees and expenses incurred in connection with the arranging, or documentation, of the Equipment Lease.

D. *Timetable*

SunTime Corporation will adhere to the following time schedule in connection with evaluating submitted proposals, making the award decision and negotiating the equipment lease document(s):

Action	*Date*
Lessor Proposal Intent Notification Due	
Lessor Proposals Due	
Lessor Proposal Commitment Cut-Off	
Lessor Notification of Initial Qualification	
Form Lease Document(s) Sent to Qualified Lessor(s)	
Lessor Response to Form Lease Document(s)	
Lessor(s) Selection	
Award Announcement	
Lease Negotiations - Start	
Lease Signing	
Anticipated Equipment Delivery	
Anticipated Equipment Acceptance for Lease	

Sincerely,

SunTime Corporation

By: _____

Its: _____

About the Author

Richard M. Contino, Esq. is an internationally recognized attorney, equipment leasing advisor, seminar instructor, and a businessman, experienced in the legal, business, marketing, and financial aspects of equipment financing. He is a Managing Director of First Lease Advisors, an equipment leasing and financing consulting firm; a Managing Director of Fairfield Capital Group, LLC, an equipment lease syndication firm; and the Managing Partner of Contino + Partners, a law firm whose practice is limited to equipment leasing and financing. He has an LLM (in Corporate Law) from the New York University Graduate School of Law; a Juris Doctor from the University of Maryland School of Law; and a Bachelor of Aeronautical Engineering from Rensselaer Polytechnic Institute. He is a member of the Bar of the State of New York and has been admitted to the Bars in the State of Maryland and the District of Columbia. Richard Contino is also a member of the American and New York State Bar Associations and is listed in Who's Who of American Law, Who's Who of Emerging Leaders, Who's Who in the World, and The International Who's Who of Contemporary Achievement. He is the author of the following books and book material:

- COMMERCIAL LAW AND PRACTICE GUIDE, LexisNexis Matthew Bender, 2008, 2018 (Revision Leasing Editor)
- New York Commercial Law (2012 Edition), LexisNexis Matthew Bender (UCC Art. 2A Chapter Author)
- THE COMPLETE HANDBOOK OF EQUIPMENT LEASING, AMACOM Books, 2002 and 2006; Second Edition, 2015
- ASSET-BASED FINANCING, LexisNexis Matthew Bender, 2006 (Revision Tax Editor)
- THE COMPLETE BOOK OF EQUIPMENT LEASING AGREEMENTS, AMACOM Books, 1997

- HANDBOOK OF EQUIPMENT LEASING, AMACOM Books, 1989; Second Edition, 1996
- NEGOTIATING BUSINESS EQUIPMENT LEASES, McGraw-Hill, 1995, Second Edition, 1998
- LEGAL AND FINANCIAL ASPECTS OF EQUIPMENT LEASING TRANSACTIONS, Prentice-Hall, 1979
- THE FRANCHISING HANDBOOK, AMACOM Books, 1993 (Finance Author)
- TRUST YOUR GUT! - A Practical Guide to Developing and Using Intuition for Business, AMACOM Books, 1996

Index

OTHER TITLES IN THE BUSINESS LAW AND CORPORATE RISK MANAGEMENT COLLECTION

John Wood, Econautics Sustainability Institute, Editor

- *Conversations in Cyberspace* by Giulio D'Agostino
- *Cybersecurity Law: Protect Yourself and Your Customers* by Shimon Brathwaite
- *Understanding Cyberrisks in IoT: When Smart Things Turn Against You* by Carolina A. Adaros Boye
- *How New Risk Management Helps Leaders Master Uncertainty* by Robert B. Pojasek
- *AI Concepts for Business Applications* by Nelson E. Brestoff
- *Equipment Leasing and Financing* by Richard M. Contino

Announcing the Business Expert Press Digital Library

Concise e-books business students need for classroom and research

This book can also be purchased in an e-book collection by your library as

- a one-time purchase,
- that is owned forever,
- allows for simultaneous readers,
- has no restrictions on printing, and
- can be downloaded as PDFs from within the library community.

Our digital library collections are a great solution to beat the rising cost of textbooks. E-books can be loaded into their course management systems or onto students' e-book readers.
The **Business Expert Press** digital libraries are very affordable, with no obligation to buy in future years. For more information, please visit **www.businessexpertpress.com/librarians**. To set up a trial in the United States, please email **sales@businessexpertpress.com**.

www.ingramcontent.com/pod-product-compliance
Lightning Source LLC
Chambersburg PA
CBHW061213220326
41599CB00025B/4629